EVERGREEN PILOT BOOKS

BERTOLT BRECHT

UNIVERSITY OF THE PACIFIC
1851
STOCKTON, CALIFORNIA

BERTOLT BRECHT

Ronald Gray

GROVE PRESS, INC.
NEW YORK

First published by Oliver and Boyd Ltd
Edinburgh, Scotland, 1961

Library of Congress Catalog Card Number: 61-9100

First Evergreen Edition 1961

Manufactured in Great Britain

CONTENTS

ACKNOWLEDGMENTS

Acknowledgment is due to Methuen and Co., Ltd, for the quotations from *The Threepenny Opera* on pp. 48 and 49. All other quotations from the works of Brecht have been translated by the author, and acknowledgment for permission to reproduce them is due to Suhrkamp Verlag, Frankfurt am Main.

Acknowledgment is also due to *Encounter* for permission to quote from the article by Herbert Luthy.

R.G.

ABBREVIATED TITLES BY WHICH BRECHT'S WORKS AND SOME OTHERS ARE CITED IN THE TEXT

Brecht's Works

P.	=	*Plays, Volume I.*
S.	=	*Stücke.*
S.T.	=	*Schriften zum Theater.*
T.	=	*Theaterarbeit, Sechs Aufführungen des Berliner Ensembles.*
V.	=	*Versuche.*

Others

Adler	=	H. Adler, "Bert Brecht's Theatre."
Benjamin	=	W. Benjamin, "Was ist episches Theater?"
Esslin	=	M. Esslin, *Brecht, a Choice of Evils.*
Grimm	=	R. Grimm, *Bertolt Brecht. Die Struktur seines Werkes.*
Lüthy	=	H. Lüthy, "Of poor Bert Brecht."
Mennemeier	=	F. N. Mennemeier, "Brecht: Mutter Courage und ihre Kinder."
Rohrmoser	=	G. Rohrmoser, "Brecht: Das Leben des Galilei."
Schumacher	=	E. Schumacher, *Die dramatischen Versuche Bertolt Brechts 1918–1933.*
S.F. 1	=	*Sinn und Form*, Sonderheft Bertolt Brecht.
S.F. 2	=	*Sinn und Form*, Zweites Sonderheft Bertolt Brecht.
Willett	=	John Willett, *The Theatre of Bertolt Brecht.*

For further details, see the Bibliography on p. 115 ff.

CHAPTER I

LIFE AND TIMES

Bert Brecht, later to become the leading dramatist of Germany after the Nazi War, was born on 10 February 1898 in the ancient city of Augsburg, in what was then the Kingdom of Bavaria. The revolutionary developments in society which were to transform Germany and to be a main impetus to his life's work had then scarcely begun. Bismarck's Reich, uniting the German states in a way unknown before in all history, had been in existence for twenty-seven years, and an almost incredible growth of political and economic power was under way. Within some forty years of the foundation of the Reich, the population of Germany grew from 41 to 65 millions, while at the same time the nation was transformed from one of peasant farmers and skilled craftsmen into the chief industrial nation of Western Europe. There was an immense influx into the industrial areas: where before two-thirds of the population had lived in the country, within this same period two-thirds of it ended by living in towns, and with this came a corresponding growth in the Socialist vote, which rose from 124,000 in the early seventies to over four million in 1912. Yet Nietzsche's criticisms of 1873 still held true. The new society was in the main a sham, a smug, uncritical, optimistic product of pedantic schoolmastering, which paid lip-service to "Kultur" and was ultimately concerned more with economic prosperity than anything else. It was also a chauvinistic society that enjoyed hearing the sabre-rattling of Wilhelm II, that paid more respect to the military caste than to any other, and that was finally to dash with enthusiasm into the opening stages of the First World War. A good deal of Brecht's later devotion to the Communist cause can be understood better against this background of ruthless capitalism, nationalism, and pseudo-greatness in his early youth.

Augsburg was then still a quiet, idyllic place. What Brecht detected under the surface cannot be known, except perhaps for one memory which he records: the enthusiasm and almost veneration felt there for a local murderer. Here already, in Brecht's revolt against this concealed masochism or sadism, was a forecast of the topic which he later made peculiarly his own: the detestation of the hero who is at the same time a "great" criminal, the attempt at weaning his public from a hero-worship which was in reality a subtle means of self-indulgence. And if Brecht was morally so strongly repelled by this, the influence of his early religious upbringing should not be left out of account. He was the son of a mixed marriage: his father a Roman Catholic, his mother a Protestant, which may in part explain why he never in mature life held any Christian beliefs. Nevertheless, for a professing Communist, he was concerned with problems of morality and virtue in an unusual way, and it is recorded that on one occasion, being asked what literature had had the strongest influence on his work, he replied: "Don't laugh. The Bible." This should not conceal the fact that Brecht could be outspoken in his denunciation of religion, and of Christianity in particular. Yet when the "Good Woman" of Setzuan, in one of his last plays, addresses her Chinese gods in a desperate appeal, the religious side of Brecht himself comes clearly to the fore:

"Something must be wrong with your world. Why
Is a price set on wickedness, and why is the good man
Attended by such harsh punishments?"

It might well be a reminiscence of the Psalms that brought forth this passionate outburst, and while the tenor of the play as a whole is decidedly anti-religious, its premises are curiously close to the discontent which is at the basis of all religion.

Brecht's attitude here, which singles him out from the general run of Communist writers, is no doubt a part of that "petty bourgeois" upbringing for which Communist critics take him to task on other counts. He did not spring from the working class—though he might have been none the less religiously concerned if he had—but from a fairly well-to-do family. His father was managing director of a paper-mill, his mother the daughter of a civil servant, and although on both sides he traced his ancestry back to "peasants" (a term which may mean anything in German from a labourer to a prosperous farmer), his upbringing was that of a reasonably well-off young man, not a "son of the people." He attended the public elementary school from 1904 to 1908, as the vast majority of German children always do, and from 1908 to 1917 the *Realgymnasium* at Augsburg, roughly corresponding to an English grammar-school of the day, although with more emphasis on modern languages and scientific subjects. In 1917 he completed this normal career by entering the University of Munich as a student of medicine and natural science, only to be called up for military service in the following year. The consciousness of the comparative sedateness and middle-class quality of this upbringing was never to leave Brecht's mind completely. His leading Marxist commentator, Ernst Schumacher, finds in it the source even of his excessive protestations on behalf of the Communist cause. Thus when, in *The Measures Taken*, Brecht condemns the young man who seeks to alleviate the lot of the poor on compassionate grounds, rather than wait until the dictatorship of the proletariat brings a more general relief, it may well be that he is condemning also his own charitable tendencies and his inability to accept the party line more wholeheartedly. Or again, when his "St Joan of the Stockyards," the Salvation Army lass who seeks to do good to the poor of Chicago, realises her inadequacy, she may be once again expressing a part of Brecht's own thoughts: "I must go. What is done by violence can't be good. I don't belong to them. If I had been taught as a child by the kicks of misery and the force of hunger, I should belong to them and not ask questions. But as it is I must go."[1] It is true that in both these plays Brecht ends by coming down on the side of violence and even brutality. Yet their themes, which are the overcoming of an initial resistance to such violence, must reflect something of his own problems.

One early story from Brecht's schooldays does, however, throw light on a particular facet of his personality that has not so far been touched upon. It is related by a friend that Brecht and another boy were at the bottom of the class in French and Latin respectively, and ran the risk of being kept down at the end of the school year. The latter tried to improve his position by erasing some of the corrected passages and presenting a rewritten copy for a revision of his mark. The ruse was soon discovered and a box on the ears was the only result. Brecht noting the lack of success of this approach to the problem, adopted more original tactics. He underlined in red ink a number of additional passages in his own work, took these to the master and asked how they came to be marked wrong. The master, unfamiliar with this particular dodge, confessed that he had been over-stringent, increased the mark, and Brecht moved up to the next class.[2]

There are traces here of the ironic servility which Martin Esslin has styled Brecht's "Schweikian" attitude, after the character in Jaroslav Hašek's novel, *The Good Soldier Schweik*. Schweik never protests, never attempts to assert his own will to gain his ends; he acts rather in the manner of a ju-jitsu wrestler, who allows his opponent's weight to work to his own advantage. By complying with regulations somewhat in the spirit of strikers who "work to rule" he both shows up the absurdity of the regulations and more often than not escapes with profit. So Brecht here did not assert his right to a better mark; on the contrary he made himself out to be worse than he was, suggesting to the master that a false estimate had perhaps come from a false expectation. By assuming the part of the dunce to an even greater extent than had been overtly allotted to him, he secured a revision of his case. Similar tactics occur over and over again in the characters of Brecht's plays. Galileo the recanter might have been chosen purposefully as the type of those who live to fight another day. In the battle of *The Horatii and Curiatii* it is precisely the warrior who runs away who is thereby able to dispatch his outnumbering opponents as they come up singly, already wounded and strung out at various distances by their various speeds. Pelagea Vlassova, the agitator in Brecht's adaptation from Gorki, *The Mother*, is highly skilled in taking over her enemy's arguments as if they were her own, and thereby revealing their inadequacies. Yet while these devices often smack of the Marxist dialectic—indeed *The Horatii* is meant as an introduction to the meaning of the term—it is not clear whether this adaptational technique is always presented as admirable. The fact that "Mother Courage" adapts herself to her environment so successfully proves in the end to be her undoing, and it is the quixotic, almost pointless protest of her daughter Kattrin that stays in the mind as an inspiration when the play is over. Galileo's subtlety does, it is true, enable him to put on a show of complete subservience to the Roman Church, while at the same time producing the *Discorsi* which the scientific world eagerly awaits. But in Brecht's productions of the play, this subtlety was both allowed its due measure of esteem, while also the refusal to make any overt protest was condemned with extraordinary passion. One has the impression that Brecht was divided on this issue. On the one hand there was his natural peasant slyness, which often bore good fruit. On the other there was his unusually strong sympathy with virtue exercised for its own sake, regardless of consequences. Especially in his later work, this sympathy shows itself time and time again. *Galileo* is concerned with devotion to truth, *Mother Courage* with bravery, self-sacrifice, and devotion to duty; *The Visions of Simone Machard* gives a notably sympathetic portrayal of a young girl's patriotism, modelled on Joan of Arc, who more than once had a fascination for Brecht; *The Good Woman of Setzuan* is a play about the possibility of good deeds, *The Caucasian Chalk Circle* is one about justice. All these, and some others besides, reveal a dichotomy in Brecht, a continual inner dialogue between the claims of absolute goodness, right, justice on the one hand, and a chameleon-like adaptation on the other. In his life, the chameleon was on the whole to gain the upper hand, as we shall see. In his work, the demands of virtue are constantly reasserting themselves.

Brecht served in the army for something under a year, as a medical orderly. The gruesome scenes of a military hospital were to leave their mark on his poetry, especially that of the twenties. They left little on his dramatic work, apart from a general and strong aversion to war such as is seen in *The Trial of Lucullus* and *Mother Courage*. It is a curious fact about the plays that, although a number of them deal directly or indirectly with warfare, none are harrowing as war-plays often can be. It is almost as though the older Brecht had drawn a curtain over his horror, which shows clearly enough in his poems, as he did at times over his compassion, although no doubt for different reasons. Be that as it may, Brecht returned from military service with no illusions about human nature and the atrocities it is continually capable of committing. He returned to a Germany in the throes of despair. The Reich, which had seemed the seal of German superiority, had vanished in a few days, leaving in its place chaos, disillusionment, and, in some cases, a cynical determination to restore the country to military greatness at whatever cost and by whatever means became available. There were widespread unemployment, inflation, starvation rations, and a constant threat of national disintegration for years to follow. Almost the only determined opposition to a renewal of militarism came, meanwhile, from the newly-constituted Communist party, whose leaders Rosa Luxemburg and Karl Liebknecht had already been assassinated in the early days after the Armistice. It needs to be remembered, for the understanding of Brecht's later adherence to the Communists, that while Ebert, the newly appointed President, was negotiating with the German General Staff for the continuance of an already corrupt tradition, it was the Communists alone who refused to accept the blandishments of a professedly democratic régime. What they had to put in the place of actuality might, it is true, have proved no better in the long run. For Brecht in his early twenties, at all events, it must have seemed as though there was only one party in real opposition, and that this demanded his support.

The support was not to be plainly given, however, for another decade. During the twenties Brecht's attitude towards the Party must often have been that expressed by the returned prisoner of war in his first performed play, *Drums in the Night*, refusing to participate in the Spartacist uprising of early 1919: "Do you think I'm going to rot in the gutter so that what you call the Idea can keep on the up and up? What's the matter with you, drunk?"[3] Certainly, until *The Measures Taken* was performed in 1930, there was no explicit reference to Communism in any of his dramatic works. If anything, Brecht was an anarchist up to that time, an anarchist not so much politically as morally and emotionally, accepting no conventional order in any sphere. He married in 1922, and was divorced five years later. He became "*Dramaturg*" (a kind of dramatic adviser and editor) at the Munich Kammerspiele in 1920, and worked later under two of the leading producers of the times, Max Reinhardt and Erwin Piscator; his personal methods of production were, however, a continual and deliberate outrage on the susceptibilities of his audiences. Following the example, to some extent, of the anti-art movement known as "Dada," among whose members he counted some close friends, he cultivated a mystique of sport, associating with a well-known boxer, careering round Berlin (where he had now settled) in a fast open car, and declaring that the theatre must offer entertainment not of a solemn seriousness, but in the spirit of the boxing-ring and the race-course. Art had become altogether too holy for Brecht's liking, and perhaps it needs some acquaintance with dyed-in-the-wool Wagnerians to appreciate the intensity of his revolt. The theatre was full of Expressionist plays that proclaimed in tones of frenzied ecstasy their faith in Mankind, in the New Man who was supposed to be in his birth-pangs after the recent Armageddon, in the Inexpressible, the Super-vital, the Super-individual, in Identity with the Cosmos, Identity with Everybody. In reaction, Brecht had his hair cut in a straight line across the top of his forehead, a style that has since caught on with all deliberate anti-sentimentalists. He wore clothes that approximated to a factory worker's working rig. He hung notices round the auditoriums advising his audiences to "Stop goggling like a lot of Romantics." He wrote plays in which there was no trace of the New Man, but, at the most, violently exaggerated satire of the type of society which had produced him as an ideal. And he cultivated jazz and an American terseness. It was this that led to his first outstanding success. By the time *The Threepenny Opera* was produced in Berlin in 1928, Brecht had had half a dozen plays performed, almost always in the teeth of violently indignant protests. Within a short time of the first night, his name was known all over Germany, Kurt Weill's jazzy tunes were being whistled everywhere, and slogans from the play such as "Eats first, morals after," became catchwords of the day. It was an extremely popular work, for all the wrong reasons. Brecht's intention, as he wrote afterwards, had been to write "a kind of report on what the spectator in the theatre [*sc.* the bourgeois spectator] likes to see of life":[4] it was a piece of Schweikian irony, meant to say to the public, "This is the kind of thing you like. How do you like it?" The answer was that the public did like it, and the borderline between self-indulgence and self-criticism was hard to draw, if possible to draw at all. The success of Brecht's anti-Romanticism, anti-sentimentalism, anti-operatics was thus a doubtful one. Positive social message the play seemed to have none, or no clear one, and it was hard to see, on his own terms, whether he had written a smash-hit or a failure. All the same, *The Threepenny Opera* put Brecht for the time being among the forefront as well as the *avant-garde* of German dramatists.

It was also at this time that Brecht became known as a poet, with the publication of his *Domestic Breviary* in 1927, a collection of ballads, lyrics and satires which earned the name from a Roman Catholic critic of "The Devil's Prayer-book." Strongly influenced by Rimbaud, Villon, and Kipling, they revealed a cunning simplicity, a preoccupation with the grotesque and with corruption, and a precise sense of values in diction—nor are they as diabolical as might be thought at first glance. They have not the naked simplicity of some of Brecht's later poems, and indeed there is little space in a book of this length to say more than that Brecht was capable throughout his life of writing poems of enduring worth. Something of this may become apparent in the verse quotations from his plays, but a full appreciation of Brecht's poetic work would obscure the main outlines of his dramatic productions. It may also be added here that Brecht's essays in novel-writing, the *Threepenny Novel* of 1934 and *The Business Deals of Mr Julius Caesar* of 1957 were not particularly successful, though his *Stories of Mr Keuner* (1930–1956) are entertaining and provoking.

Meanwhile, the time of chaos was drawing to an end. Germany had barely emerged from the inflationary period after the war into relative economic stability when it was plunged again into disorder by the world depression of 1929. This in itself, as a clear sign of the irrationality and wastefulness of the capitalist system, was enough to turn Brecht's thoughts more strongly to the Communist offer of a solution. At the same time, capitalism seemed to him and to many other Left-wing intellectuals to be entering on its ultimate stage in the growth of Nazism. The Nazi Party, with the support of financiers and press-magnates, took advantage of the depression to capture the imaginations of millions of supporters with the promise of an organised society which should be self-supporting, thoroughly German, and no longer subject to the vicissitudes that had oppressed the nation for the last decade and a half. It first emerged as a power in the land when it gained 112 seats in the Reichstag election of 1930. Whether these factors in fact influenced Brecht it is impossible to say: it seems likely, but there is no concrete evidence at present to show for it. (Indeed, in the absence of any fully-documented biography, all accounts of Brecht's life must be regarded as provisional.) What is certain is that his own explicitly Communist plays date from just this period of economic depression and the threat of a tyranny such as Germany had never known before.

It was also in this period that he began to have his plays performed by proletarian organisations. *The Measures Taken*, a play dealing with Communist methods of agitation in China, was first performed in 1930 by the Workers' Chorus of Greater Berlin. *He who said Yes*, a piece which advocates also the complete subordination of the individual to the interests of the community, even to the point of requiring his death, was performed by schoolchildren in the same year. And early in 1932 came the adaptation from Gorki's novel, *The Mother*, in which the Communist cause is enthusiastically taken up by a shrewd, wily, humourous, yet passionately convinced woman of the working class who has, in character, a good deal in common with Brecht himself. (The part was in fact played by, perhaps written for Helene Weigel, whom Brecht had married in 1928 and who remains to this day the outstanding exponent of his dramatic practice.) Of these three plays the first two are remarkable for their ruthless rejection, even omission, of any claims made on behalf of individuals. In their one-sidedness they give the impression that Brecht was determined to persuade himself by violence of the need for violence; it is as though, faced with the threat of Nazism, he was resolved to conquer his pacifistic sentiments and make common cause with those who were bent on meeting force with force. (Nor should it be forgotten that almost the whole world was driven to this expedient against Nazism in the end, although without exercising on individuals quite the totalitarian discipline that Brecht apparently sought to have imposed.) The third play, meanwhile, although decidedly a propagandist work, is saved from the didacticism of the other two by the Brechtian humanity which shows through the character of the "Mother." The acute problems of the Communist convert are not touched on here, the question of ends justifying means never arises, while at the same time, and for the first time in all Brecht's work to date, the Russian Revolution is explicitly and emphatically held up as a model for workers in Germany.

It was a long step from the *Threepenny Opera,* with its mixture of wit, facetious clowning, brash popular numbers, occasional sharp prickings of the audience's conscience, and ultimate vagueness and irresponsibility, to this downright propagation of an ideal. What was more, it was almost too late. Performances of *The Mother* were banned in public, and within a year the catastrophe had come and the Nazis had achieved their "bloodless" seizure of power. In 1933 Brecht was forced to fly from

Germany, his books already, like those of so many others, under a ban. He came near to worse tragedy when his two-year-old daughter Barbara ran the risk of being held as a hostage within the country and was saved only by the precarious rescue operation of an English welfare worker—an event which can give more poignancy to the somewhat similar story incorporated in his later play, *The Caucasian Chalk Circle.* But although his family remained intact, with his wife and both their children restored to him, Brecht did not take the obvious step that he might have been expected to take. He did not go to Russia. Instead, after a period of moving through Austria, Switzerland, and France, he settled in Denmark, where he remained, apart from visits to Paris and New York made mainly in order to see performances of his plays, from the late spring of 1933 till the summer of 1939. He did not, of course, make any break with Communism, and there could have been a variety of reasons why he chose to remain outside the central places of the movement. In fact, however, although he became co-editor of *Das Wort*, the refugee periodical published in Moscow, he made only one visit to the Russian capital and—if the report is true—explained his failure to stay there with the smiling excuse, "I could not get enough sugar for my tea and coffee." This may have been before, during, or after the notorious treason trials of 1937, and the sugar may have referred to sweetness of various kinds. At all events, Brecht found no permanent attraction in Russia, and his later movements give rise to even more curious speculation. On the eve of war, Brecht left Denmark for Stockholm, and later, in 1940, for Finland. From there, almost on the Russian frontier, he applied for and received a United States visa, which he used on 21 July 1940 to enter the U.S.A. through California. He had, in fact, for what reasons can only be guessed, elected to travel across the entire length of the Soviet Union only to emerge at the other end at Vladivostok and sail to safety across the Pacific. Small wonder, then, if it has been supposed that his allegiance to Communism was less than whole-hearted. It may not have been so. Brecht may have felt he had better work to do through his contacts in non-Communist countries. Or he may have felt, what seems most likely, that while Communism was still his aim it could not be realised under present circumstances, and that he had better work to do than would be permitted in Communist countries. Whatever the case, however, Brecht's journeyings in exile do not suggest the kind of man who was as ready to submit to Party discipline as his propagandist works of the early thirties would lead one to suppose.

Nor, for that matter, do the plays of the exile continue the propagandist strain. Such as do have a propagandist element—*Round Heads and Pointed Heads*, *Fear and Misery in the Third Reich*, *Señora Carrar's Rifles*, all written by 1937, are rather anti-Nazi or anti-Fascist than specifically pro-Communist. After this, in fact, Brecht was to treat explicitly of Communism only in three works (apart from short poems)—in the "realistic," un-Brechtian prologue to *The Caucasian Chalk Circle*, in the treatment of a famous Communist failure in *The Days of the Commune*, and in the generally deplored cantata of the post-war years, *Herrnburger Bericht*, which has all the air of a sop to conscience. It really looks as though, having overreached himself to conform in the early thirties, Brecht had seized on the Communist opposition to Nazism as one feature of which he could whole-heartedly approve, and channelled his propagandist work along that course. Meanwhile, from 1937 onwards and until 1941, he set about writing the plays which have most established his reputation abroad: *Mother Courage*, *The Life of Galileo*, *The Good Woman of Setzuan*, *Herr Puntila and his Man Matti*. (*The Caucasian Chalk Circle*, belonging with these in style, was written later, from 1944 to 1945.) These were works of a quite different kind. It is possible, though not logically necessary, to read out of them the corollary that only Communism can cure the ills they represent. Their general sphere of interest and concern is not, however, directly political, but rather one of general humanity. They are plays in which the spectator is implicitly invited to consider the behaviour of human beings, to understand, sometimes to sympathise, sometimes to be revolted, and always to ask himself how he might have acted in similar circumstances. There are no incomprehensible farragos or flippant shocks for shock's sake such as occur from time to time in the plays of the twenties, nor are there any choruses ramming home the "message," as there are in the plays of the early thirties. No one is counselled to do evil so that good may come. Instead, there is an essentially humane theatre, tolerant yet insistent on justice, offering comprehension rather than persuasion, ranging in mood from tender lyricism to agony of mind, from admiration for the most insignificant details of ordinary living to a buffooning zest in wine, women, and song, from sharp compassion with the miseries of the poor to a not wholly unsympathetic portrayal of the pleasures of the rich. It is the "human comedy" that Brecht seems most of all bent on showing in these works, and the Communistic implications are at most a side-issue, for all that he may have thought otherwise. What brought about this second change in him is once again hard to determine with the knowledge at present available. Whether the grief of exile tempered the passions and increased understanding, whether the suddenness of Brecht's conversion to outspokenly Communist views in the early thirties brought an inevitable reaction, it is impossible to say.

Nevertheless, the new plays do reflect a change which was evident in Brecht when he returned from the United States after the war. He had not lost his old sly humour, nor his passionate concerns. To say that he had become mellower is likely to give a false impression if it conveys the idea that he had grown into a second Olympian

Goethe—and the legend that seeks to place him on a pedestal with the great German whom he detested has already begun to take shape. Brecht wanted no pedestals for anyone. But the scroll containing a portrait of a Chinese sage, which he had carried about all through his exile and still retained, does give some clue to his ideals, and it was not for nothing that he wrote, apparently during the war, scenes for a play on the life of Confucius. The "human-hearted" philosopher, also an exile, with his this-worldly religion, his unassuming ways, his attempts at transforming the "Great Society" of China, and his adaptational approach to most human problems, had a good deal in common with the later Brecht. A greater tolerance was noticeable in him than had been seen before; he sat easy to the world, despite the fact that he was still bent on changing it out of all recognition, and there are many tributes from technicians, workmen, actors, and actresses both to his sharply critical attitude and to his willingness to adapt every situation and every talent to the best end in sight. Moreover, Brecht's view of the function of the theatre had changed. It was no longer to be directly political, but rather, as he wrote in the *Little Organon* of 1948, a place in which the worker might "enjoy his terrible and never-ending labours as entertainment, together with the terrors of his ceaseless transformation."[5] In short, it was fundamentally an aesthetic philosophy with which Brecht had returned: "the easiest form of existence is"—not in the proletarian state, apparently, or that only incidentally, but—"in art."[6] A contemplative attitude is thus yoked with the revolutionary one that Brecht still maintained, and it is often difficult to see how they can truly have kept in step.

This is in fact the chief problem of Brecht's final years. He settled in East Berlin in 1949, having made a visit there a year earlier, and was to remain there, apart from trips abroad, for the rest of his life. He had made his choice, and though the Democratic Republic was not perhaps the realization of his ideal, he preferred it to the capitalist framework in the Federal Republic of the West. At the same time, he apparently took good care, by acquiring a passport of Austrian nationality, that he should not be limited by the restrictions that were to be expected, and his bank account was in Switzerland. He never had to make use of these precautionary loopholes, as it turned out, yet the fact that he arranged them indicates where his thoughts were running. He was prepared, evidently, to make the adaptation necessary for a return to that part of Germany which, he hoped, would at last make reasonable use of the industrial revolution that had begun shortly before his birth. But he foresaw the possibility that the course of events would end as it had done in Russia, and he needed the assurance of a possible backdoor exit if he found himself in the long run unable to compromise. Compromise was in fact forced on him on at least two notorious occasions. First, in 1950, *The Trial of Lucullus* was withdrawn after one performance, and subsequently alterations were made which seriously affected the libretto's uncompromising pacifism. This was done at the request of the government, and it is not clear what kind of pressure was used to obtain this end. Second, in 1953, there was the popular uprising in East Berlin of 17 June, suppressed ruthlessly by Soviet military forces. On this occasion Brecht wrote a long letter, allegedly containing some criticisms of this action, of which only the final sentence declaring his "attachment to the Socialist Unity Party" at this critical moment was published by the party newspaper. That he was humiliated by this selective editing seems beyond question. That open criticism of a totalitarian régime is self-imposed martyrdom is equally obvious. The fact remains that there is no utterance of Brecht's on record in which he makes any protest at all against governmental iniquities. He is said to have sympathised with the reformist plans of Wolfgang Harich, who was later sent down for a long prison sentence, and he certainly believed, late in life, that Communism had been "only hinted at, never put into practice."[7] But, on the whole, the self-preserving chameleon-attitude which enabled him, like his own Galileo, to pay lip-service to authority while quietly getting on with his own serious interests, remained predominant.

It is a question which this study may partly answer, whether martyrdom or adaptation was the better course —a question which Brecht had already done something to answer in his own treatment of the recanter, written long before its applicability so his own case could have been foreseen. So far as Brecht's own life was concerned, there was much to be gained by compromise. The theatre at the Schiffbauerdamm in Berlin, where many of his earlier plays had been performed, was placed at his disposal in 1954, and from 1949 onwards he began to build up the Berliner Ensemble for special performances of his own works and adaptations from the classics. It was an opportunity for practical experimentation perhaps too good to be missed, and two phrases used by Brecht at rehearsals remain in the mind as indications of the mood in which he took it. "I'm not trying to show that I'm in the right, but to find out whether." This was humble language in contrast with the dogmatism of earlier days. And again, this time to an actor, "To blazes with the play, it's your turn now." Nothing Brecht had written was sacrosanct; if the occasion demanded it whole speeches could be inserted, new characters invented, sometimes even whole scenes concocted to put right some defect that stage-production had revealed. He sat easy to his own work as he did to the world at large, tinkering at it, bringing it closer to reality, rather than making it the bearer of an imposing idea. And in this "dialectical" aproach to the theatre, keeping his work constantly in a state of flux, lay Brecht's most important contribution to the post-war Communist world. Marxism is very much a philosophy of adaptation to circumstances and careful observation of reality; if these qualities have been obscured in recent times, that is because it has become, as Christianity once became, a rigid system of dogma. Brecht's virtue is that he broke up the rigidity and thereby restored the system to some of its former dynamic force. The fact that he was able to persevere in the production of plays that were avowedly Marxist in content, and yet so obviously anti-doctrinaire in spirit, may mean that the fresh winds already being allowed to blow faintly in Soviet literature have also a chance of making themselves felt in Eastern Germany. So at least Brecht may have thought, and some pretext for his shameful compromises may be found in that. On the other hand, the idea that totalitarian régimes can be treated as schoolmasters can, as though they had some regard for rules of fair play, is deceptive. Since Brecht's death from coronary thrombosis on 14 August 1956, shortly before the visit of the Berliner Ensemble to London, there has been little sign of a real willingness on the part of the East German Government to allow Brecht's voice to be heard in its full and natural tones. Already in 1954, the first night of *The Caucasian Chalk Circle* was ignored by the party newspaper *Neues Deutschland.* The "Brecht Archives" in East Berlin clearly contain a great deal of material that has not yet been published, and which the custodians, Brecht's relatives and friends, are circumspect in making known even to *bona fide* researchers, perhaps out of anxiety that too many of his views may prove unpalatable in governmental circles, once they become public property. And in this thought lies one of the weightier arguments in the discussion, whether more is to be gained by outspoken protest or a policy of calculated risks. For in the long run the totalitarian government has the whip hand. It may tolerate a nibble here and there at its foundations, but from the moment any serious attempt at change seems in the offing it has only to tighten its grip, and it is as though nothing had been said. Brecht was not popular with either Eastern German governmental circles or with Soviet Russian critics. That he was tolerated is probably a sign that his works were not felt to be particularly dangerous. Whether, if allowed still to be read and seen, they will contribute to the framing of a more humane attitude, is a question that still remains open.

REFERENCES

1. *S.*, IV, p. 158.
2. *S.F.*, I, p. 5.
3. *S.*, I, p. 187.
4. *S.*, III, p. 141.
5. *V.*, 12, p. 140.
6. *ibid.*
7. *S.*, VIII, p. 199.

CHAPTER II

CRITICS AND PRODUCTIONS

The debate on Brecht's work involves some questions of largely German significance and some of much wider and more general import. What Brecht has to say about acting and the reactions of audiences in theatres has more to do with the conditions he found on the German stage than with those current in France, Britain, and the U.S.A. The form of play he advocated, the "epic," or, as it has also been called, the "open" drama, can also be understood in part as a reaction against the classical drama of Goethe and Schiller, and as an affirmation of the tradition represented by such dramatists as Lenz, Büchner, the early Hauptmann, and Wedekind. There is no space to go into this tradition here. Brecht at once becomes internationally intelligible, however, from the moment that his purposes as a whole are considered.

The last hundred years or so have seen in Europe and America the crystallisation of at least two major attitudes or "philosophies" in relation to the world at large: on the one hand an attitude which accommodates to the prevailing conditions, on the other an attitude which seeks to change them—in brief, to adopt Arthur Koestler's convenient if over-simple classification, the attitude of the Yogi and that of the Commissar. Neither attitude is new in the world; there have always been stoics, mystics, quietists, contemplatives alongside revolutionaries, utopians, reformers, and missionaries, and this could scarcely be otherwise, for if we were entirely occupied in making plans for the future we could probably not endure living in the present, whereas it is precisely an acceptance of the present, however tragic or horrifying, that contemplatives usually aim to achieve. However, the current forms which these attitudes take are worth recalling to mind. We have seen a remarkable growth in the last sixty years of philosophies and techniques of accommodation, ranging from the near-mystical "abandonment" of Rilke, to the efforts of psychologists to induce integrated personalities who will come to some sort of terms with the societies in which they live. In Britain, the dominant trend in philosophising has aimed at the removal of unnecessary worries; its purpose has been largely therapeutic, and one of its best-known pronouncements has been to the effect that "philosophy leaves everything as it is." The later plays of T. S. Eliot, in a different way, have also reflected on and to some extent condoned the tendency to go on with the cocktail party. In the U.S.A. a trend which goes back to Emerson has emerged again in the cult of Zen Buddhism, encouraging the ritual drinking of tea while the house falls in ruins all around. And in Germany, above all, philosophies of acceptance have been the rule since Goethe sent the soul of "damnable Faustus" soaring to heaven in the teeth of all his moral failings and human inadequacies. A generously tolerant tradition which ultimately, after negative criticism has been allowed its run, affirms the rightness of the world order on all counts, runs from Goethe through Hegel and Schopenhauer, in a yet more modified form through Nietzsche and Heidegger, and finds its latest representative in Thomas Mann.

The effects of this tradition have been disastrous in Germany, for all the subtlety and variety with which it has been expressed. Young German intellectuals conscripted into the Nazi armies might be revolted at the barbarities which they knew to exist—in fact they were revolted, as their published letters show.[1] But they looked back to a line of thinkers and poets in whom they could find assurance that the very worst that might happen was a part of the divinely or naturally ordered scheme of things, to be accepted and endured not for the good that might come of it, but because it had to be—and they went on fighting tenaciously till Berlin was in flames and every major German city was in ruins. How far they were justified in interpreting their tradition in this way is a question beyond the scope of this book to investigate. It was, however, against such an interpretation, and against the parallel interpretation of Christianity as a religion of resignation, that Brecht formulated his own dramatic practice and theory. He regarded all such attitudes as symptomatic of the decadence of the "bourgeois" world, and attacked in particular the conception of the theatre as a place where the public might rid itself of those emotions which would otherwise lead it to demand that the world be changed.

The situation became complicated, however, by the fact that Brecht very soon declared his allegiance to the political movement which has asserted more insistently than any other the propriety of events, at least of those events which occur inside its own dominion. So far as the Communist world is concerned, the Commissar *is* a Yogi, and Brecht himself did not escape writing the adulatory ode to Stalin or the banal glorification of Soviet society which this circumstance requires. As a result, the debate on Brecht has been very largely a political one. The questions asked about him have not been, in the main, what precisely are the effects achieved by his plays, what qualities they show, what they achieve best and what least well, in short how they stand as plays, as wholes, but rather, in the words of Martin Esslin, "how far is it possible to be committed to a political creed and yet to produce works which, like all of the greatest literature, are of universal validity and appeal to all mankind?"[2] This question, it is worth noting, takes it for granted that Brecht's plays do belong to the greatest literature, and indeed Mr Esslin claims that his book "tries to see Brecht . . . as a great dramatist and a great poet, one of the greatest of our time."[3] Yet Mr Esslin nowhere makes sufficiently clear what this greatness is, and devotes only one third of his book to an examination of the works in themselves, as works of literature. Here he argues that the "real meaning" of Brecht's plays runs counter to the author's expressed intentions;[4] that the audiences who saw in Mother Courage "an embodiment of the eternal virtues of the common people,"[5] and thus presumably ignored the qualities of ruthless selfishness and blind greed which Brecht was careful to include, were in the right despite his protests. For the rest, he is concerned with biographical matters, the discussion of Brecht's political allegiance, and suggestions regarding the connexions between Brecht's personal psychological problems and his work, interesting topics in themselves, but unrelated to the central issue he has formulated. One can read through this whole book without being helped to come to any opinion about whether Brecht's work really deserves the high praise it has been given. The same is true of John Willett's highly valuable collection of material relating to Brecht's background, literary forebears, development, and ideas. For while Mr Willett takes issue with Mr Esslin over the emphasis to be placed on Brecht's political beliefs, and insists that Brecht was first and foremost an artist, he too does not attempt to demonstrate that he was or was not a great artist. There is nowhere in his book a coherent critical account of any one play, or any reasoned assessment of Brecht's achievement based on such an account. There are incidental comments, but no more. Eric Bentley, who has done a great deal to introduce English-speaking audiences to Brecht's work, has restricted himself so far to a general discussion of the nature of his plays and theories taken in the lump. In fact, while the word "great" has been widely used in Britain and America to describe Brecht's quality, there has still been no large-scale attempt in English at explaining it. The adjective has passed from mouth to mouth with a tacit assumption that connoisseurs would recognise its aptness.

The situation on the Continent is not essentially different. The French studies by René Wintzen and Geneviève Serreau are informative rather than critical, and have been superseded in their own sphere by Mr Willett's detailed account. The larger studies in German, meanwhile, have tended to devote themselves to the purely scientific categorising of different aspects, a method which is useful for indicating Brecht's originality, his indebtedness to the past, the general coherence of his work, and for defining its place in literary history, but which still leaves the vital question unbroached. Peter Szondi, in an influential study of the theory of modern drama, has sought to show that the form of Brecht's plays answers to a condition of contemporary living: that Man has recently become aware of his own nature in a new way and that this "objectivising of Being" requires the formal development of an "epic" theatre where Man confronts himself in a critical mood. This approach provides a good example of the historical method of criticism which is practised more widely in Germany than in other countries. It has the advantage that it insists on seeing a work within its historical context, and the disadvantage that it determines or assumes values in terms of that context: it provides no means of distinguishing between works which show the formal features common to their epoch but vary in respect of quality. Similarly Reinhold Grimm, who confirms Mr Szondi's findings in some respects, is mainly concerned with analysing the dramatic, stage-technical, and linguistic devices of Brecht, and with showing that all of them may be classed under the general heading of "*Verfremdung*," or "estrangement" effects. His study provides a unifying picture of the nature of Brecht's work which is questionable in some ways, since he extends the term "*Verfremdung*" to cover many devices of poetry which have been common in all ages; nevertheless he indicates a number of features which would be missed at a more superficial level of attentiveness. But, once again, no estimate of any single work or of the treatment of individual parts is offered, and one is left with the feeling that a similarly unifying picture could be produced by this method of almost any author one cared to examine. The same is true of Volker Klotz's often perceptive study with its significant sub-title, "An Essay on the Work": the singular noun shows that it is the work, the *œuvre* as a whole with little regard for its patches of success and failure, or for its variations of mood and intention, rather than the individual works, which concerns the author. The peculiar quality of a work of art, which can be marred by a false phrase at a vital moment, escapes notice under these conditions. So it is also with Walter Hinck's study of Brecht's later dramatic theory and practice: examples are culled from a range of works of widely differing effectiveness and arranged so as to provide a definition of the "open" form of drama; from this Mr Hinck proceeds to show that this "open" form corresponds to certain sociological developments within the last century, and examines other manifestations of it in the work of Thornton Wilder and Paul Claudel. He concludes by suggesting some interesting parallels between Brecht's work and the Protestant drama of the Reformation on the one hand, and between Claudel's and the Jesuit drama of the Counter-Reformation on the other. Yet the significant point escapes his attention, that both these earlier forms of drama are today dead wood, the works themselves never performed except on rare occasions in a spirit of piety. They served their didactic turn and belong now to history: must it be argued that Brecht's and Claudel's work is equally limited?

In contrast to these more academic studies stands Franz Mennemeier's essay on *Mother Courage*, in a volume containing essays by various hands on the classic German repertory. This is an account based on the analysis of particular details which does attempt to define the sheer dramatic qualities of Brecht's art. It tends, it is true, to look for the "meaning" of the play, as something that can be reasonably summarised in a few words, and it finds this meaning in a deep apocalyptic pessimism that seems to have more kinship with the philosophy of Heidegger, or the theology of his adherents, than with Brecht. It is the "lament at the transitoriness of existence and at the vanity of the works of men, good and bad alike,"[6] which Mr Mennemeier finds at the heart of this play, a conclusion which, like Mr Esslin's, needs at least to be defended against the charge that it does not accord with Brecht's own utterances. Nevertheless, there is much useful material here about the structure, the language, and the theatrical effectiveness of some parts of the play. It would be pleasing to say the same of the other essay on Brecht in the same volume: Günter Rohrmoser's study of *The Life of Galileo*. But here, despite the fact that one play only is studied, the argument concentrates almost entirely on "meaning," on discussing the problem raised by the play as though it were a geniune historical study, a philosophical essay, or a treatise on morality. Inevitably Brecht's plays arouse such discussions. The fact that they do so, however, says nothing at all about the value of his plays as plays. And even less is said by the pedantic polemic against Brecht by Professor Otto Mann.

The writers mentioned in the last two paragraphs all publish their work in the Federal Republic. The picture from the other side of the Iron Curtain is rather different. It is true that the Polish critic Andrzej Wirth shares the approach of his Western colleagues in his study of the "stereometric" structure of Brecht's plays, a study which has been aptly criticised in Mr Hinck's book. It is, however, a Marxist critic rather than any other who has provided the most discriminating account of Brecht's work, play by play, that has yet appeared. Ernst Schumacher's massive volume is restricted to an account of the plays written up to 1933; a treatment of the later plays has yet to appear. It is a mine of information on the German political theatre of the twenties, on the attitude of contemporary critics and theorists towards Brecht's works, on the conditions of performance, and on details of the productions. At the same time, Mr Schumacher finds space for detailed and enlightening comment on each individual play; he distinguishes wheat from chaff and does not engage in generalisations abstracted from particular contexts. His criteria, it is true, are those of the Marxist-Leninist, and will not carry the same authority with all readers. Yet they do often correspond in function to those which a non-Marxist might want to apply. Thus, in writing of *St Joan of the Stockyards*, Schumacher points out the incongruence of the dying heroine's violent attack on religious believers; here is a play, he argues, whose whole trend seemed to be directed towards social criticism of the capitalist system: to switch this criticism in the final scene to an attack on religion is to ignore the principal task confronting the Communist party. Schumacher's point here, if its insistence on incongruence is isolated from the political application, hits on a feature of the play which will probably strike critics of all professions. In purely literary terms, the noting of the incongruence is enough; Schumacher, however, relates it to a system of political thought. And so, while his references to official doctrine will often seem rigid and on some occasions even stultifying, there is also in his book much material for thought on the issue formulated by Mr Esslin. It is certainly possible by means of it to arrive at some conclusions about Brecht's quality as an artist judged by Communist standards, and to some extent also, though indirectly, about his quality judged by more generally human ones.

It is a matter of some consequence that Schumacher's assessment, incomplete as it is, has already made its appearance, for without it there could be no possible meeting-place for conflicting opinions. Those critics who deny Brecht's title to greatness have in fact done no more to substantiate their views than those who advocate it. Nevertheless, the mere fact that a contrary view has been expressed makes the need for substantiation on one side or the other more urgent. Herbert Lüthy, for example, has criticised Brecht's work in the strongest terms: "[Brecht] himself has never really created a plot: debating scenes, the puppet theatre of the didactic pieces, sketches and loose sequences of scenes in cabaret or revue style seem to mark the limits of his own powers of dramatic construction. All his figures . . . have the same quality of stubborn immobility, the same cocoon-like inner and outer loneliness."[7] It is as a great director rather than as a great dramatist, in Mr Lüthy's view, that Brecht has made his mark. Henry Adler takes a similar view of a play which many others have taken to be Brecht's masterpiece. Writing of the climactic scene in *Mother Courage*, where the dumb girl Kattrin sounds a drum-tattoo to warn a sleeping city of impending attack, he finds in it only sentimentalism and the "hammiest melodrama," and adds: "Sentimentalism does indeed break completely loose in the final scene, which shows the demented solitary woman heaving the wagon while lightning flickers, thunder rumbles, and the wind and her nerves scream in a piece of 1920 expressionism which badly lets down the control and restraint which the play has so carefully tried to adopt."[8] This may or may not be true; I think it is not true. The point is that the debate has not centred on issues like these, and for all that has been written on the later plays there is almost no critical writing to which one can turn for an evaluation of them. Sentimentalism is a difficult thing to define; Mr Adler's recorded impression, partly wrong as to the facts (Mother Courage is not, for instance, demented), and stated without any indication of the context, does not in itself establish that sentimentalism is present. And yet, until questions of this kind come to the forefront, the debate on Brecht cannot really be said to have begun. Critics have inevitably ranged themselves according to their first impressions, and sides have been taken very largely in proportion to the sympathy that has been felt with Brecht's iconoclasm and demand for social change. Scholars have applied themselves to elucidations and categorisations as they would do in the case of an established classic, and researches have been carried out into the theatrical history of Brecht's times. But all this has been done as though the question of value could be left to popular acclamation, or shelved until a historical perspective could be gained by later generations. It is almost pointless to ask whether it is possible to be a Communist and a great artist at one and the same time, to discuss the implications of Brecht's theories, to compare his formal developments with those of his contemporaries, or even to argue the pros and cons of the moral and social problems raised by some of his plays, until some firmer impression can be gained of his achievements in the particular field he chose to work in: the drama. To provide an impetus towards gaining that impression, and to suggest the necessity for focusing attention on the dramatic rather than on the political, biographical, social, psychological, and moral aspects of Brecht's life and work, are among the main purposes of this short book. This can only be a beginning, and it will be useful to bear in mind throughout the literary critic's best *vade-mecum*, the thought that he may be wrong. But on these terms some approach at least is possible to the Brecht who affirmed that he was not trying to prove himself in the right, but "to find out whether."

One feature of these works, however, needs special emphasis. Less than the plays of any other dramatist can Brecht's plays be appreciated by reference to the printed text alone. This, as Brecht said, "gives scarcely more than the prompter's copy of a piece that has been entirely handed over to the theatre."[9] His full intentions did not become apparent until he had worked over the play in the light of experience gained at rehearsals, and they could never be called complete or final. From his earliest days he was accustomed to inserting new scenes, altering lines, and even handing out bundles of new speeches to every actor, sometimes as late as the dress rehearsal.[10] Moreover, the stage "business" which grew out of this contact with the living theatre, especially through Brecht's experience with the Berliner Ensemble, could often add details, conveyed entirely by gesture and expression, of which no trace is to be found in the text. Thus, in *The Caucasian Chalk Circle*, a young peasant girl has saved a baby from death during a revolution, and is making her way with it across dangerous mountains to her home. She stops by an isolated hut to buy milk, only to be asked an exorbitant price for it by a grasping farmer, which at length, after some haggling, she pays.[11] The scene, two pages long, is interesting in the printed version for the rough humour of the peasant-girl, her "dialogue" with the baby explaining why it can have no milk, and her gradually-won consent to the farmer's price: the farmer himself has little to say and appears a mere type of tight-fisted exactingness. In the Ensemble production, directed by Brecht, however, a great deal more is added, and the scene becomes more humanly rounded. The farmer appears first suspiciously round the door of his hut, fearful of the plundering soldiery in the neighbourhood: his cautiousness with any stranger begins to be explained from the outset. On seeing the fine clothes worn by the baby (it is in fact the child of a provincial Governor) his suspicion increases: the rich are likely to prove unwelcome. Yet when the child is given its milk he relaxes and shows some pleasure: an ordinary human feeling bridges over the difference of social class, and in this one expression alone an indication is given of where Brecht really stood politically. Finally, when the feeding is over, a complete small episode, still not incorporated in any book, is added. The girl still has the child in her arms, her heavy bundle is still on the ground where she laid it, and it is next to impossible for her to pick it up. And here —you can see the action being built up at rehearsals out of the difficulties of the actress—a further sign of human feeling shows itself in the farmer, who lifts the bundle and helps the girl to settle it on her shoulder. What might have been merely a producer's device for getting an actress off stage without awkwardness, however, is built into the scene as a whole: it is used to illuminate more of the farmer's underlying character. As the girl leaves, her back turned to him, he lifts the empty can to his lips and tilts it as high as it will go, on the chance that a drop of milk may be left. There is greed once again, but at the same time an awareness of the extreme necessity where a drop of milk needs to be so carefully used. From the whole episode, meanwhile, there emerges a picture in which the spectator is constantly being reminded of the claims of charity and of the reasons why they are not met, a flow of interest, critical judgment, sympathy and reflexion whose extent might not be guessed from the text alone.[12]

The stage itself is also used to underscore the moods of plays and to achieve effects which the theatre alone can provide. There are a few lyrical moments in *The Caucasian Chalk Circle*, moments when the action pauses, and the narrator, sitting close to the audience, turns from prose to a lilting verse enjoyable for itself alone. Yet one of the most memorable effects of the Ensemble productions of this play was in the retaining of an incident that would once have been hidden from sight by the front tabs. A huge white backcloth, suspended mid-stage with plenty of room on either side towards the wings, had represented on it a steeply rising mountain-village in Georgia. It was not, however, lowered slowly and mechanically into view, or secretly placed in position while the audience was excluded. Instead, it billowed down freely from a great height in swathe after swathe, and was allowed to sway to a standstill in its own good time. The sight was beautiful in itself, for all that it was incidental to the play and might even have come about initially through a stage-hand's negligence. At the same time it was integrated into Brecht's total purpose. It served to bring home at least momentarily the theatricality of the scene, in other words to "estrange" the play in accordance with Brecht's theory. And in addition, coming as it did as the prelude to a scene of bloody revolution, it acted as a reminder of the beauty that goes on existing side by side with horrors. Nowhere but on the stage could this particular effect be achieved or even thought of. Similarly, the activities of the rogue cook in *Mother Courage*, a man whose scheming and sometimes ruthless character is an important element in the play, were seen in a new guise by the mere fashion in which he prepared a meal. His chopping of carrots held in mid-air so that the sliced orange discs spun off one after the other into a bucket below was dwelt upon sufficiently long to draw attention, while also with sufficient tact not to remind one awkwardly of the "dignity of labour" announced by Soviet theorists: and here once again the beauty of the scene was ranged alongside the squalid stage-action required by the printed word. Unspoken commentaries such as this, scattered through the play, could have done much to counter the impression gained by some critics, perhaps unaware of them, that the play must convey an unrelieved pessimism. And Brecht was in any case not solemnly devoted to these devices. It was part of his policy to insist on the theatricality of the stage, but he could also subject the policy to deliberate and genial ridicule. In *Drums and Trumpets* a scene in a library required a character to consult a book; the bookshelves and books, however, in accordance with Brecht's anti-naturalistic demands, were painted on free-standing flats, so that it might have become necessary to have the required volume lying on a table in front. In Brecht's production, a space had been cut away from the canvas of the flat, and a real book placed along with the painted backs, which the actor selected and produced with a flourish of triumph. The episode recalled Mozart's inclusion of a snatch from *Figaro* in *Don Giovanni*; a piece of self-parody that was not only amusing in the comedy but a reminder not to adopt any of Brecht's techniques in a merely imitative spirit.

The style of acting in the Ensemble, and more particularly the care and thought that went into it, was a further elucidation of Brecht's intentions; it had a clean-cut, unsentimental matter-of-factness that is certainly required by his language as a rule, yet which does not always translate itself in non-Brechtian productions. Mother Courage's first entry on her covered wagon, drawn by her two sons, with her daughter Kattrin sitting on the step, is a case in point. In the Ensemble version the mother lolls back almost luxuriously against the canvas flaps, one arm extended along the curved roof: she is grinning to herself with some satisfaction. The sons are striding out smartly, in step, the simple, kindhearted, thoroughly honest Swisscheese showing rather more determination than his brother Eilif, who has more of a swagger, and a slightly abashed smile. Both are plainly soldiers already in wish and imagination; they may have to pull their mother's cart for the time being, but their minds are on the future, and if Swisscheese overdoes the part, that is because Eilif will in fact prove the better fighter. Eilif, meanwhile, already shows by his smile some awareness of the absurdity of his future career, an absurdity which will become more pronounced as the play continues. Dumb Kattrin, behind the brothers on the step, glances apprehensively to one side, crouched a little over her mouth-organ. She too is playing her part in the family business for the moment, but something of the protest she is to make is already apparent in her bearing. In this way the four parade round the stage, leaving the audience to receive its first impressions of the characters it is to meet for the rest of the evening: every detail of gesture and motion has been thought out to lend emphasis to the purely verbal aspects of the work. A complete contrast to this was provided by the B.B.C. Television production of 1959. Here, the general positioning was almost identical, with roughly the same wagon, the women on the step, and the young men at the head of the shaft. Mother Courage, however, sat upright, chin slightly raised, eyes proudly and fondly cast down towards her sons, mouth cheerfully singing to the music of Kattrin, who was also smiling. The sons toiled manfully: Eilif with a slightly rueful smile, his eyes lifted to some distant horizon, Swisscheese with one shoulder determinedly thrust forward and a wistful good humour in his expression. On the whole, the actors showed here a general appreciation of their roles. Swisscheese had been seen as the kindly son, well-intentioned, and this characterisation emerged in each action. Mother Courage was the woman who cheerfully endured the worst, the embodiment of eternal virtues admired by Mr Esslin and denied by Brecht, and again this single aspect dominated the actress's interpretation. There were thus no surprises, or rather no surprises for the unreflecting, and considerable surprises for spectators who looked for some consistency. Where Mother Courage and her sons are so well-disposed, it is not at all clear how, later in the play, they come to be so cynical on the one hand, or so blindly trustful on the other. Their continued endurance in war becomes incomprehensible: they are people with high ideals, tragically beaten down by an inscrutable, external fate, instead of human beings observed in the round, detesting war and desiring it, cynically decrying their own potential and yet surprisingly showing extreme heroism and devotion, each ignorant of his own most fundamental urges whether towards good or evil. Brecht's actors in themselves reveal a good part of his meaning. The grin of Mother Courage and her lolling body are indications of the enjoyment she has from her trading off the war, while the very fact that her expression is a grin and not a smile suggests the slight uncertainty that accompanies this mood. Swisscheese's pursed lips reveal the naivety with which he will join the Protestant armies, fully convinced that virtue will bring its own reward, while Kattrin's apprehensiveness is in itself a comment on these illusions. The acting establishes a sympathy with these characters as human beings, while at the same time it promotes a sense of the folly and on occasions the wickedness of their activities, and this dual mood is perhaps the best definition of the general trend of Brecht's later plays that can be given for the time being. From the billowing-down of the backcloth to the chopping of carrots, from the action of the farmer lifting the girl's load on to her back to the calm innocence of Swisscheese, there is a pervasive sense of justification, not to say "acceptance" of the world, which stands in contrast to the sometimes savage denunciations that Brecht unlooses against many of his characters. The combination can perhaps never be exactly defined except by the actual performances of the works as Brecht intended them to be played. Its presence may, however, be indicated by occasional references.

The high quality of Brecht's productions has drawn attention to his work in recent years, regardless of the plays performed. It is still another question, what qualities his own plays have in themselves, whether his achievement is that of a producer or a playwright. The sketching of an answer to this question must be the main concern of the remainder of these pages, and it is as well to say in advance that Brecht was a long time in maturing. The earlier plays, while it is important to have a knowledge of them in order to appreciate the significance of some features in the later ones, record a struggle of some twenty years' duration, during one of the most disastrous periods in German history, both to remain receptive to the currents of the times, and to establish some personal pattern that would yield dramatic wholes. The traditions of thought, both literary and philosophical, into which Brecht was born rendered his task all the more difficult.

REFERENCES

1. See *Kriegsbriefe gefallener Studenten*, edd. W. and H. W. Bähr, Tübingen 1952.
2. *Manchester Guardian*, 24 Nov. 1959.
3. *ibid.*
4. See, *e.g.*, Esslin, p. 206.
5. Esslin, p. 204.
6. Mennemeier, p. 312.
7. Lüthy, p. 47.
8. Adler, p. 119.
9. *S.*, III, p. 141.
10. *S.F.*, 2, p. 432.
11. *S.*, x, pp. 177–8.
12. See also *S.F.*, 2, pp. 322–36: "Brecht probiert."

CHAPTER III

EARLY PLAYS

The post-war Germany in which Brecht wrote his first plays was a chaos, whether seen in social or in literary terms. For the *avant-garde*, one movement alone was of real importance: Expressionism, with its ecstatic, visionary, staccato style, its revelling in gruesome horrors, its self-consciously orgiastic frenzies, and its programme of "expressing" the essence of the cosmos. Until the late twenties, Brecht's work was to remain within this atmosphere, and his first play, *Baal* (1918), is in some ways, not all, an epitome of it. Baal, its central character, is at once a lyric poet, a practical joker, a murderer, a homosexual, a violent lover who prefers having two women in bed at a time, a cynic, a helper of elderly women, a reveller in sensual pleasures of every kind, the one forthright and outspoken man in the whole play, and yet one without conscience or self-knowledge, a teeming mass of contradictory qualities who lives his life at an intense level of enjoyment. Yet *Baal* does not leave in the mouth the taste of the general run of Expressionist plays; it is shocking and repellent, but not self-conscious or bathetic, and there are passages in it of lyrical tenderness that lend a kind of innocence to the ugly wickedness it portrays. It has been summarised as expressing "a passionate acceptance of the world in all its sordid grandeur,"[1] but the phrase has something high-falutin about it which makes it immediately inappropriate. For it is precisely such an acceptance that was expressed by the play which gave rise, by reaction, to Brecht's play: the romanticising tragedy by Hanns Johst, *Der Einsame* (*The Lonely One*).

Johst's play, published in 1917, consists of a series of episodes in the life of the dramatist Grabbe, a contemporary of Heine's; evidently influenced by the current vogue for Rimbaud, it presents, like Brecht's, a kind of glorification of the poet's untrammelled life. Grabbe shudders in ecstasy, frequently weeps, is unfaithful to his dead mistress, is ruthless, egotistical, misunderstood, and lonely, but he is inspired:

> Oh! This feeling! Not for a throne would I exchange it! This God-the-Father feeling! Heaven and earth dependent on my favour! I am the cosmos![2]

On his deathbed, Grabbe gives vent to the feeling of which so little has been seen in his life, a versified "Dionysian" welcome to all existence:

> Oh, [*He sits up, feverishly*]
> How gay it all was, in memory how fine,
> Heaven and friendship, loving and wine!
> Suns on the mountains, the flowers and grass,
> Spring and the winter! Still dancing they pass,
> Laughing and weeping! Sorrow and joy!
> Shudders of bliss in the heart of a boy!
> Cursing and praying! Aloneness! Yet twain
> See the splendour of endless world-glory again![3]

The poet sinks back, the weight of this splendour proving too much for him; pressing his hands folded in prayer against his heart, he seeks to quell its beating in humble acceptance of death. And as he lies in death, his friends enter through the window to serenade him with the "booming chords" of a Beethoven quartet, observing without sense of irony that "a German poet sleeps soundly and well." The play is full of the clichés of Expressionism, banal and conventional despite its pretended fervours. Most young poets were in favour of passionately accepting the world, living a Nietzschean life of intoxicated splendour, declaring themselves free of moral and social ties. Brecht's play, written as a retort to Johst's, differs in that Baal is seen enjoying the pleasures of which Grabbe only speaks, and in that Baal is a genuine criminal, not merely an ungrateful son or a faithless lover: in good and evil he is real. Only quotation, however, can bring home the contrast briefly and adequately. Baal's death-scene contains, thematically speaking, much the same ideas as Grabbe's, but in an entirely different tone. Here is Baal, weak with some undefined illness, lying on the ground in a forest hut, surrounded by woodcutters:

A MAN: You old woman! There's something to think about! [*Spits in his face. All move to the door.*]
BAAL: Stay for twenty minutes. [*Men exeunt through open door.*]
ONE OF THE MEN [*at the door*]: Stars.
BAAL: Wipe the spittle off.
THE MAN [*going to him*]: Where?
BAAL: On my forehead.
THE MAN: There. What are you laughing at?
BAAL: I like the taste.
THE MAN [*angrily*]: You're a back-number, that's what you are. Au revoir. [*Takes axe and goes to door.*]
BAAL: Thanks.
THE MAN: Is there anything else I can—but I've got to get to work. Crucifix. Corpses!
BAAL: Hey there! Come closer. [*Man bends down.*] It was wonderful....
THE MAN: What was, you crazy cockerel, or I should say capon?
BAAL: Everything.
THE MAN: Fancy tastes you've got. [*Laughs loudly, exit; the door stays open, blue night-sky is seen.*]
BAAL [*anxiously*]: Hey there! Man!
THE MAN [*at window*]: Huh?
BAAL: You going?
THE MAN: To work.

BAAL: Where?

THE MAN: What's that to you?

BAAL: What time is it?

THE MAN: Quarter past eleven. [*Exit.*]

BAAL: He's gone to the devil. [*Silence.*] One, two, three, four, five, six. That's no good. [*Silence.*] Mum, tell Ekart to go away, the sky's so damned close you could touch it, everything sopping wet again. Go to sleep. One. Two. Three. Four. It's stifling here. Must be light outside. I'll go out. [*Gets up.*] I will go out. Dear Baal. [*Sharply.*] I'm *not* dying like a rat. Must be light outside. Dear Baal. Still get to the door. Still got knees, it's better in the doorway. Damn! Dear Baal. [*Crawls on all fours to the threshold.*] Stars . . . . hm. [*He crawls outside.*][4]

There is nothing passionate about the acceptance here, rather a dryness, a reflective appreciation that expresses itself in the final grunt. Baal is neither heroic nor stoical, but amused and analytical in these last moments, for all that he has been passionate at other times. He realises that he would prefer not to be alone now, but his reception of the men's refusal is without self-pity, and the language in general has a crispness and lack of sentimentality. Only in Baal's monologue does his fundamental narcissism show clearly—he loves himself in everything he does, as he loves the spittle and the stars—but even this has a terseness that restrains the suggestion of a cosmic self-identification. There is also, perhaps, something formally stylised about the staccato exchanges, something that recalls the so-called "telegraphese" of the Expressionists, and these laconic utterances betray a lack of ease. Yet the quality of this language was refreshing enough, after the fustian of almost every other German play of the time, to win over some hearers at least to an appreciation of Brecht's talents. As for the play as a whole, despite its rambling structure and lack of concern with any character save Baal himself, Brecht had set down a picture of an amoral life which was in the main ruthless in its consistency. He had shown that such a life as Baal's was a possibility, although a monstrous and revolting one. He had drawn the consequences of a Nietzschean philosophy without the sentimentality common among his contemporaries, without Nietzsche's torturous self-analyses, and had added an acceptable tender note of his own which marked him off distinctly from any cult of the Superman. As a retort to Johst, *Baal* had succeeded. There remained, however, further questions, and as a sign of the times *Baal* was immensely disturbing. The play was, after all, a fantasy, a modern and harsher version of the Romantic Eichendorff's *Good-for-Nothing*, and its consistency, relentless as it was, remained in the sphere of fantasy. It showed what the life might be of a man who gave free rein to every impulse, and was never touched by that regard for other men's rights and lives which comes inevitably to anyone who lives in society. Having killed his best friend in a fit of rage, Baal afterwards finds the event no more than interesting: his indifference, in real life, would border on insanity. Thus there is a sense in which Schumacher is right to speak of an "escape into Bohemianism."[5] Yet there was also an indication in the structure of the play that Brecht himself adopted an amoral attitude towards his character, that he accepted him without demur and even prized him more highly than the more humdrum characters in whom he had taken so little interest. *Baal* might well be taken, perhaps was meant to be taken, as the manifesto of a new humanity which for the time being at least appealed to Brecht, a humanity in accordance with many trends of the time, untrammelled by moral conventions of any kind and devoted to a hedonistic indulgence in the most intense experience. If that were so, Brecht's literary talent, his crisp language and clear-sighted vision within the sphere he chose to write about might prove a menacing omen.

By the time *Baal* had been brought to the stage, the Nazi movement was already under way. But, then again, Brecht's frankness was surely enough to preserve him in the long run from the self-infatuated cult of that barbarism. In fact it was Johst who became a Nazi.

Baal stands alone among Brecht's plays in its total lack of any social relevance: the Baal-figure was scarcely to reappear again in his work until the late thirties, when it could be seen, modified, in such characters as Puntila and Azdak. Of the other early plays which followed in rapid succession, all take some cognisance of society, whether to accept or reject its claims. *Drums in the Night* (1918–20) explores the reaction of a returned prisoner of war to the abortive Communist revolution of 1919, and shows him decisively rejecting it. *In the Cities' Jungle* (1921–4) is the first of a longish list of plays in which conditions of life in capitalist America are portrayed in grotesque caricature. And even the adaptation from Marlowe's *Edward II* (published in 1924) gave the play a curious contemporary political significance. Despite this, however, the impression given by the first two of these plays remains one of amoral, neutral recognition. The returned prisoner makes his choice, preferring individual happiness to sharing in social revolution, but it is not obvious that his attitude is being recommended. Rather, as a friend wrote at the time, Brecht was gripped by the horror of the times, and his horror could be felt through his language on the tongue and the palate.[6] But the horror was still something to be lived through and endured, not opposed: Brecht still saw his task as a dramatist as the recording of experience in its full intensity. And so in *In the Cities' Jungle* he gave expression to the chaos inside and outside himself in a logically consistent form. *Baal* had still retained some pattern, if only in following the life of a character; *In the Cities' Jungle* is chaotic and incomprehensible. The confusion is increased by the ironical preface to the play, in which the spectator is told not to worry about the inexplicable motives of the characters but to concentrate his attention on the "finish"—advice which seems to mean that the bulk of the play is to be disregarded. Brecht reaches here almost the furthest bounds to which amoralism can come. Where neutrality is complete, there can no longer be even a structure or a connected sequence. Silence or random words seem the final alternatives, and Brecht had almost come to the point where he would have to choose between them. It is significant, therefore, that in his fourth play, *Edward II*, the principal character seeks to apply his capacity for amoral action to a useful end, the transformation of society. Mortimer in this version is a kind of early intellectual revolutionary who opposes the King in the interests of the English working class, and who finally subjects him to the foul mishandlings, mental tortures, and gruesome assassination carried out by his villainous counterpart in Marlowe. Unlike his namesake, however, Brecht's Mortimer is given a speech by which he justifies his actions. Such brutality as he has used, he affirms, was necessary for the welfare of the kingdom; he has merely taken over from the barons of the realm an odious task which had to be performed. The speech is curiously reminiscent of the "Chorale" in *Baal*, where it is said that "every crime is good for something . . . so long as you know what you want,"[7] and of several similar utterances in later plays. Moreover, there is no reply to Mortimer in the play, no counter-argument, while the King himself is made to look ridiculous in the midst of his torments, so that the whole has the appearance of a *pièce à thèse*, daring to advocate the use of torture for political ends, or at least to insist that in parallel situations the necessity for such cruelty must be recognised. The play contains in itself no indication of any other standpoint, and monstrous as the thought is, it must, on consideration, be allowed to stand as an interpretation of Brecht's intentions. As will be seen, his later, political plays make even bolder affirmations of sadistic principles.

At this point, in the writing of *Edward II*, he passed over from neutrality to the deliberate propagation of immorality in the interests of a future goal.

For some time to come, however, Brecht remained on the whole true to the Baal-like mood, accepting every condition of life without choice or conflict. It was only gradually that his concern with the lot of the working classes gave him a sense of direction and purpose, and the further emergence of this sense can be seen in his next play, *A Man's a Man* (1924–6). The theme here is still one close to Brecht's own self, that of a man who goes with the tide (a frequent image in Brecht's poems), or who, in the words of the play "aligns himself with the course of events." The treatment, however, suggests for the first time a more critical attitude. The "hero," Galy Gay, an extremely adaptable character, is here beguiled by three British soldiers into taking the place of one of their comrades in the Indian Army. Step by step, and by methods vividly reminiscent of those used today in brainwashing techniques, he is transformed from a peaceable citizen into a ferocious warrior, armed to the teeth and thirsting for blood. On this occasion, however, the events are not related entirely in a tone of "artistic" neutrality. A deliberate interruption is made by one of the characters, who advances to inform the audience of the author's intentions, and thus for the first time an element of "*Verfremdung*" or "estrangement"—a term used later by Brecht in his theoretical writings (see Ch. IV), whose sense will be seen gradually developing in these earlier works—is clearly introduced.[8] Yet the intentions, for all that, are not made particularly clear. There is some concern, it is true, about the possibility that a character like Galy Gay can be so transformed:

> They'll soon, if we don't watch over him
> In the wink of an eye make a butcher of him.[9]

The imperialism caricatured in the play is plainly denounced. At the same time, however, a behaviouristic view of human nature is adopted, which is ultimately neutral once again. Whatever a man is made to become, the commentator continues, no mistake will have been made: his human nature is as capable of monstrosities as of what used to be called humanity. "A man's a man"—not in the sense of Robert Burns, affirming an innate value in him, but in the sense of Baal, declaring simply that he is what he is. And in the spirit of this cynicism the commentator wavers uncertainly at the end of her speech into a mere declaration that "life on earth is dangerous." In this way the ground is cut away from the moral protest that seemed about to be made, and the play proceeds on a level of ambiguity that has allowed at least two critics, mindful perhaps of Brecht's similarity to Galy Gay, to see even wisdom in the adaptability to circumstance he displays.[10] The continuing adherence to a neutralist or indifferentist view militates against the desire to affirm moral tenets, and the play leaves a bewildering impression of a ferocious irony that still leaves the standpoint of the ironist uncertain.

Equally indeterminate, and indeed strangely ambiguous, despite the lucid and racy style which contributed a good deal to its popular success, is *The Threepenny Opera* (1928), a libretto presenting an analysis of capitalist society, and based on Proudhon's dictum that property is theft. For this, Brecht took over the basic situation and some of the scenes from John Gay's *Beggar's Opera*, and made of the highwayman Macheath and his associates not a parody of leading statesmen of the day, such as the eighteenth-century work had presented, but representatives of bourgeois capitalism. Here already a note of indeterminacy entered the text. Gay's work had been both demoralising, in the opinion of Defoe, and highly entertaining, in the opinion of Boswell; the satire, however, was definite in its reference, and everyone recognised in Lockit and Peachum Sir Robert Walpole, then

Prime Minister, and Lord Townshend, who had recently quarrelled.[11] Brecht's opera proved equally entertaining, but its satire was directed at nobody in particular. Macheath was intended for "the" bourgeois businessman,[12] an abstraction who could not readily be detected in the lively, unconventional, almost Baal-like figure that Brecht made of him. Indeed, while Macheath's robberies were presented as parallels to the normal activities of rentiers and bankers, they did not always appear to be as reprehensible as Brecht's comments suggested. The amoral aspect of the play emerged in such lines as "What is burgling a bank compared with founding one?" and "Eats first, morals after." At the same time, Macheath himself, despite his role as a bourgeois, was required to express the attitude presumably meant for that of the Communist party: it was he who incited the audience to "smash the faces of the police with heavy iron hammers."[13] In a text so full of irony, it becomes difficult to see what is being ironised. In one aspect, Brecht appeared to have written a work demanding a social revolution, in another, he appeared to have satirised the revolution itself.

On the other hand, there is a note of compassion running through the opera which contrasts oddly with all that has been said of it and of Brecht's work so far, a note that is announced at the outset by the employer of professional beggars, Peachum:

> Something's got to happen. My business is too difficult, you know why?—because it's my business to awaken human sympathy. There's a few things that shake people, a few, but the worst of it is, once you've used them a fair number of times, they don't work any more. Because people have this terrible faculty of making themselves feel nothing at all, more or less when they like. For instance, if a man sees another man with one arm standing at a street-corner, he'll want to give him a shilling the first time out of sheer fright, but the second

time it'll be sixpence, and the third time he'll hand him over to the police in cold blood. It's just the same with these religious gimmicks. [*A large placard with the words* "IT IS MORE BLESSED TO GIVE THAN TO RECEIVE" *descends from the flies.*] What's the use of the most beautiful, the most earnest texts, painted on the most attractive placards, when they get used up so fast? There must be four or five texts in the Bible that touch your heart; once you've used those, there's nothing in the kitty. . . . You have to give 'em something new all the time. The Bible will have to fish something out again, but how long is that going to last?[14]

There is already a new device of Brecht's in this speech whereby a character speaks direct to the audience, outlining his own situation, a device which he was to use for purposes of "*Verfremdung*" frequently later on. With this, there enters a note which also recurs in the later plays a number of times: the statement of a religious standpoint expressed with such irony as to seem an attack on religion. On closer inspection, however, it is seen that this also is a device, serving to introduce the demand for compassion in a roundabout way. Peachum regards misery as a means of making money; at the same time his words have a ring of truth. And one of the most effective scenes in the opera is that in which Peachum parades his beggars in order to criticise the turn-out in which they hope to melt the public's heart and open its purse. The beggars are seen first in their normal appearance, a set of healthy rogues, and are transformed in front of the audience into cripples covered in sores, dressed in filthy rags, and holding placards declaring that they have suffered for Queen and Country. Nothing but perfection will do for Peachum, however. He points out that there is a difference between melting the public's heart and frightening it off: only a nicely calculated poverty will produce financial results. By this means, the audience is tacitly invited to reflect on the condition of the genuine poor who have no such expert as Peachum to instruct them. Here the technique of "*Verfremdung*" has been developed a further step: the scene depends for its effect not on the direct participation of the audience in the happenings on stage, which are deliberately "acted out," but by their reacting from them and remembering more forcefully the true state of things.

The cynical recognition of facts, already observed in Brecht's earlier plays, thus acquires a new edge in this opera. Each of the finales rounding off the three acts applies it more sharply, affirming first that the world is poor, that man is bad, and that nothing can be done about it, then that crime is the basic condition of human life:

> MACHEATH: What does a man live by? By resolutely
> Ill-treating, beating, cheating, eating some other bloke!
> A man can only live by absolutely
> Forgetting he's a man like other folk!
> CHORUS [*off*]: So, gentlemen, do not be taken in:
> Men live exclusively by mortal sin.[15]

The lines spoken by the chorus here might have been spoken by Baal; thanks to the "*Verfremdung*" devices, however, they have a different ring. They are now quite clearly meant both to be an objective appraisal, and also to arouse a reaction through shock. The brief glimpse of what human nature might be, in contrast to what it is, that appeared in *A Man's a Man*, becomes a longer look. It still does not, however, provide insight into the theme of the opera as a whole, which retains a dual aspect, partly amoral, partly charitable, as a brief glance at the last finale will show. Here, Macheath is saved from execution, as he is in Gay, by a last-minute pardon from the King, which is greeted with exaggerated relief as the sign of a "happy ending," and the irony is apparent enough. Villains are pardoned in real life as well as on the stage, "capitalist villains" in particular, and by providing the public with its favourite entertainment Brecht comments cynically on its taste. Yet the sung finale itself, in which the whole cast advances to the footlights, accompanied by organ-music, is not so plain in intention. Free pardons from the King, Peachum has just declared, very seldom come when the downtrodden masses have risen against their masters, and thus, he implies, Macheath and his like will not evade justice so easily in future. "Therefore," he adds, "we should never be too eager to combat injustices." Thus far, we still know where we stand, the irony is still apparent, from a Communist point of view. And even when the chorus advances, accompanied by the organ-music which Brecht used to lend a note of false solemnity, the implications remain clear for a moment:

> Combat injustice but in moderation;
> Such things will freeze to death if left alone.[16]

Yet in the last two lines of all, Brecht seems to evoke again the compassion that was ironically aroused in earlier scenes of the play:

> Remember: this whole vale of tribulation
> Is black as pitch and cold as any stone.[17]

This can scarcely be taken in a contrary sense without making nonsense of those earlier scenes. And, with this, a considerable weakness of Brecht's text emerges. Not merely is it difficult to relate his characters to the prototypes they are meant to satirise; Brecht's still "all-embracing" attitude allows him to move at will from one standpoint to another completely contradictory one: at one moment he seems to aim at arousing a general compassion for the condition of all men, at another he allows his characters to advocate extreme brutality, and the vacillation from one to the other renders every reaction uncertain. It is not surprising that his audiences, for whom he had meant to write a "report" on the kind of entertainment they liked to see,[18] seized on those aspects which took their fancy and ignored the rest. There was grist in the text for everybody's mill.

Brecht was to write one more work of this kind, *Rise and Fall of the Town of Mahagonny* (1928–9), a satire on the American capitalist way of life equally uncertain in its direction, before turning to a completely different style and subject-matter. Hitherto he had written without direct reference to the Communist cause, although with some Communistic implications. In the early thirties was published the series of plays which show him at his most unambiguous and doctrinaire. The first of these, the *Baden-Baden Cantata* [or literally, *Didactic Play*] *of Acquiescence* (1929), is uncompromising in its condemnation of all individualism, and so is the adaptation from a Japanese Noh play, *He who said Yes* (1929–30). The latter, indeed, was so absolute in its demand for subordination to a common cause as to arouse protest from the school-children who were called upon to act it, and in acceding to this criticism Brecht wrote the companion piece, *He who said No*. This, however, reduces his initial position to the platitudinous one that such subordination depends on circumstances, a point of view that was not likely to arouse much opposition. In attaching himself to a single-minded declaration of purpose, Brecht had not in fact made his position as a dramatist any the easier.

Yet this very single-mindedness was to produce strange results in *The Measures Taken* (1930), a work of remarkable simplicity of form and language, and extraordinary directness of message. The plot of this concerns four Communist agitators who have been sent to China to promote the cause of the Party, with the ultimate aim in view of bringing about a proletarian revolution. One of their number—played alternately during the action by each of the four, indicating his representativeness and restraining the audience, after the fashion of "*Verfremdung*," from self-identification—is moved by compassion rather than by faith in revolutionary doctrines. Seeing misery in front of his eyes, he cannot withstand the temptation to alleviate it, although each time that he yields, his partial reforms and local efforts achieve nothing: the workers' lot is not improved, and the position of the agitators is endangered. At length, this "emotional socialism" seems about to bring the entire mission to an end; a consultation is held, and the conclusion reached that the over-generous agitator must be killed at once, a conclusion to which he agrees in the ultimate interests of the community. There is, however, no companion-piece this time, as there was for *He who said Yes*, no consideration of other circumstances which might have led to a different conclusion. On the contrary, the action is interspersed with comments from a "control-chorus," ostensibly filling the role of a jury, which ends by declaring that the sentence of death was not arbitrary or subjective, but demanded by the realities of the situation. The whole play, clcar in outline, precise in language, has the form of a logical argument in which example after example is brought forward leading to the inevitable conclusion; and while it has displeased Schumacher, who, despite the Soviet treason trials of 1937, denies that the execution of comrades is a feature of Communist policy, it has led at least two critics to admire its "icy, inhuman greatness," and its "great emotional intensity."[19] Yet, in this play apparently devoted to reasoned exposition, scant respect is paid to the rationality of the spectator. Is it really inevitable, he may ask, that this young man should die? A pause is provided in the play in which he is invited to think this over, and in this pause he may recall the reasons already given by the agitators. They could not take the man to safety across the frontier, they declare, because they had to persuade the now aroused masses to attend political meetings.[20] Nobody suggests, in the play, that this long-term project might be put aside for a short while, or, if the immediate situation is so urgent, that the man might even manage to escape alone, or with the help of one agitator. What would happen, the agitators add, if they were to hide the man and he were to be found? They answer that there are gunboats and armoured trains which would attack any agitator they saw.[21] This again is a defeatist answer that will not consider for a moment the possibility of hiding the man so that he will not be found, or that the responsibility for his death might be left to others, while still affording him a chance of escape. There can be no emotional intensity here, for the agitators make no serious attempt at seeking a way out: not for an instant do they give the impression of urgently looking for means of saving their comrade's life, and centuries of humane tradition are brushed aside on the flimsiest of pretexts. Yet the chorus is completely convinced by these arguments, sympathising with the alleged repugnance of the agitators to their inhuman task, but affirming the correctness of their judgment, and the audience is evidently expected to share this view. The shoddiness of the reasons offered, the complete lack of any attempt at envisaging a situation in real life, can only lead one to suspect that Brecht had determined before ever writing the play to bring it to this conclusion, and that he was indifferent to the means by which its harshness was defended. The essential thing, it seems, was that audiences should be persuaded of the need for inhumanity by hook or by crook, and this despite the professed "*Verfremdung*" whereby they were encouraged to make judgments of their own.

A similar theme is treated in *St Joan of the Stockyards* (1929–31), derived from Shaw's *Major Barbara* and treating once again the problems of the "emotional socialist." Here, once again, the compassionate, in this case Christian, attempt at relieving individual suffering is contrasted with the need to "change the world." The Salvation Army heroine comes to the conclusion that where violence reigns only violence can help, and she dies with this knowledge, to the ironical accompaniment of a canonisation which expresses the very reverse of what she has come to believe. Yet in this play also a gratuitous sadism marks the concluding scenes. The heroine's last words are not directed against the evils of capitalism, as one might expect, nor do they propose any practical course of action, but rather a hysterical intolerance. Anyone who preaches the existence of God, she declares, and even anyone who claims to have any ability to rise spiritually above his material conditions, must "have his head beaten on the pavement till he croaks."[22] In a play where neither capitalists nor working classes are presented with any degree of credibility, this equally unrealistic conclusion underscores once again the effect of adherence to Communist doctrines. Brecht had once sought to grasp at a totality of human nature: now he concentrated his attention on one aspect, and a brutal one.

This was not, however, the sole result of Brecht's conversion. There belong also to this period of his writing such a brief play as *The Exception and the Rule* (1930), a moving and in some ways ambiguous plea for justice, and, more particularly, the one work which stands out above all the others of this time, the adaptation from Maxim Gorki's novel, *The Mother* (1930–31). This is a completely Communistic play, portraying the conversion of a working-class woman to the cause of the Party, and her activities on its behalf: she distributes pamphlets, takes part in demonstrations, argues with strike-breakers, gets up from her sick-bed to help the Party in its hour of need, and is seen finally holding the Red Flag aloft in the Russian Revolution of 1917. But the play is not conceived in the spirit of the purely didactic works: it does not set out to preach a direct moral or resolve a difficult point of doctrine. Formally, it has much more in common than they have with the plays of Brecht's maturity; it consists of a series of scenes loosely strung together along a common theme, rather than an organised unity tending to prove a point. In content too it has something essential in common with the later works, for the central character, the mother herself, Pelagea Vlassova, is a woman with the outstandingly vital qualities seen in Azdak, Puntila, Galileo, and Mother Courage. This vitality, as in those later works, is dramatically the most acceptable element in the play, carrying it over shortcomings. The bare narration of contents may well have given the impression of a dull work written to the Party tune, and in fact the speeches of the young revolutionaries in the opening scene set a tone of prim dedication which has first to be overcome. Enlivened by the character of Pelagea, sly, shrewd, humorous, commonsensical, forthright, and determined, the play provides a number of memorable scenes, the most notable of which, perhaps, is that in which Pelagea lines up with a queue of middle-class women to make her contribution of scrap-metal to the Russian war-effort. In Brechtian, not to say Schweikian fashion, she begins speaking, half to herself, as though her mind were running along a well-defined, conventional track: she reflects that her own contribution is small, and contrasts it unfavourably with that of other women in the queue, whose kettles and cans will provide enough metal to kill several men at once. As she continues to speak aloud the unconscious or only partly conscious intentions of her hearers, she whips them into a fury of indignation against herself. Her exact delineation of their basically murderous attitude (for all its crudity and slight unreality—the women will have had other thoughts in mind than these) like Brecht's "report" on bourgeois preferences in the *Threepenny Opera*, brings out its absurdity, and Brecht turns to good dramatic and propagandist account his habitual tendency to "guy" a situation with apparently complete solemnity. On the other hand he does not, as he unwittingly did in *The Measures Taken*, give the same treatment to the Communist doctrines which are the main propagandist theme of the play. The questionable aspects of Communism are left out of account here: there are no difficult decisions to be taken, comparable to the shooting of a Party comrade, nor is the bloody outcome of the Russian Revolution shown—on the contrary, the Revolution is presented as the glorious finale to the decisive action undertaken by Pelagea. There is, indeed, a certain idealisation of her character, despite its salty earthiness, and that Brecht recognised this is shown by his later revision of the play. Returning to East Germany after the war, he introduced a new character, an older man, through whose eyes Pelagea appeared in a new perspective.[23] In the earlier version, she had been contrasted only with younger and less efficient revolutionaries, whose callowness stood out sharply against her own shrewd appraisals. Through this contrast, however, something of a hero-worshipping attitude had entered the play: the audience was invited to admire a character whom they could scarcely expect, in view of her idiosyncrasies, to imitate. By the introduction of the older revolutionary (played by Brecht's leading actor, Ernst Busch), himself every bit as shrewd as Pelagea but with greater experience than hers, her actions became "estranged," so that while sympathy for her remained she no longer seemed the perfect model she had been. The revision is at once a confession of earlier weakness on Brecht's part, and a welcome illustration of the increasing distance from his own work that came with later years.

Of the remainder of Brecht's plays written at this time, little need be said. Two are directly concerned with the Nazi revolution: *Round Heads and Pointed Heads* (1931–4), an allegory of Nazi anti-Semitism which misfires badly, tending to show that rich Jews were the allies of their persecutors, and that the working class must oppose both; and *Fear and Misery in the Third Reich* (1935–8; also translated as *The Private Life of the Master Race*), which is in the nature of a "documentary." There was also a didactic play meant for schoolchildren, *The Horatii and the Curiatii* (1933–4), setting out the basic ideas of dialectical materialism in extremely simple form, and a naturalistic play on the Spanish Civil War, *Señora Carrar's Rifles* (1937), in which Brecht returned to the conquest of kind-heartedness in the interests of political action, this time on a more reasonable and realistic scale.

By the time he went into exile, Brecht was a famous dramatist, partly because of the success of *The Threepenny Opera*, partly because of the public scandal caused by every performance of his plays. There was a raciness and intensity about his work which can scarcely be indicated without extensive quotation, and an extremity of out-spokenness which made a violent impact. Despite the comparative absence of plot, his scenes succeed each other with a ferocious insistence; blasphemies follow appeals to charity, immorality is at one and the same time advocated and castigated, a kaleidoscope of grotesque caricatures whirls over the stage in a frenzy such as only the Expressionists were capable of, while from time to time a sudden halt is called, an appeal to reason is heard and the language reverts to a laconic terseness. In some aspects Brecht vividly calls to mind the plays of Samuel Beckett, as he does in *The Baby Elephant* (1924–5); in others he is closer to Strindberg's demonic intensity; while in others yet again he produces knockabout farce in the manner of Chaplin. His themes show affinity with Pirandello's, his formal innovations resemble Claudel's. A crowd of apparently incompatible influences throng into his work, Nietzsche and Marx, Rimbaud, Villon and Kipling; the *commedia dell' arte*, Synge and Wedekind, the Bavarian folk-play and the Japanese Noh play; jazz and Büchner, the language of the Bible and the songs of Berlin cabaret. He conducts a running fight with Goethe, Schiller, and Shakespeare, with the tradition of grand opera (to which *The Threepenny Opera* was a counter-blast), with the production methods of the best producers of his day, Reinhardt and Piscator, with the acting methods of the established school of Stanislavsky. At the same time he is continually experimenting with his own forms, thinking and experiencing in terms of theatre. Piece by piece, new elements of "*Verfremdung*" are added; the plays change shape in answer to new requirements; nothing is fortuitous, each innovation, however wild, is intended for a purpose. The sheer profusion and vitality of Brecht's work at this time, his receptivity to influences from all sides, his ability to give expression to every reaction with swift immediacy, cannot be anything else than impressive.

Yet this Baal-like openness still lives in a world of fantasy, is still centred on an exclusive self-realisation. The characters who come alive are still the central ones: Baal, the prisoner of war Kragler, Macheath, Pelagea Vlassova. The remainder are grotesques, types, mouthpieces for witticisms and cynicisms, objects of ridicule, models of Communist perfection. The depiction of social conditions, even in those plays where social criticism is intended, is wildly exaggerated: the America of *Mahagonny* and *St Joan* and the England of *The Threepenny Opera* are unrecognisable, and it is only in *Drums in the Night* and *Fear and Misery in the Third Reich* that Brecht gives anything like a picture of conditions in Germany. For the most part, the early plays contain no scenes where human beings enter into any relationship with one another, except in such a parodistic form as the friendship between Macheath and Tiger Brown. The audience is constantly being invited to draw conclusions from what it sees before it, while what it sees is presented in so biased a form that conclusions are undrawable. And when Brecht deliberately turns to the advocacy of reason in his plays, he shows so little regard for rationality as to suggest that he had never engaged in serious argument with anyone but himself.

It is a strange mixture, this unadorned forthrightness and lack of sentiment, such as is seen in *Baal*, on the one hand, this frankness and originality, receptivity and unshrinking penetration, and on the other hand this seemingly wilful blindness, inability to reason, prejudice, occasional hysteria, and preference for parody and adaptation. The mind that could produce a detailed account of the brutalities of the Third Reich in one play could give an absurdly inadequate analysis of their causes in another, and even advocate similar brutalities in others. Brecht's openness, his "all-embracing" attitude, was in fact completely uncritical, or rather critical only on the impulse of the moment, and his dramatic unities were the largely fortuitous assemblies of these impulses, able to exist side-by-side because they left out of account the continuum of the outside world. Yet the early plays do show also the ability to observe and take account of the rest of humanity. The language of the working men in *Baal*, unlike that in *The Mother* and *St Joan*, is full of idiomatic turns of phrase. The note of concern about the direction to be take by human nature enters in *A Man's a Man*, and grows louder in *The Threepenny Opera*, for all that it takes so abrupt a modification into inhumanity in the propagandist plays. There are moments of genuine emotional intensity in Pelagea Vlassova's grief at her son's death, and in the scene where parents fear betrayal by their son in *Fear and Misery in the Third Reich*. Moreover, Brecht had shown repeatedly his ability to make use of the theatre: he was no armchair dramatist but one who constantly envisaged effects in terms of theatrical performance. In *Señora Carrar's Rifles*, a priest raises his hands above his head in a reverent gesture of resignation: he is held in the act by a word, and sits there, a dramatic image of a man "surrendering." In *The Measures Taken*, the young agitator removes his mask to declare his true identity, and the physical revelation of his human personality comes as a shock which almost in itself undoes the inhuman doctrine of the play. These, with many other of the devices, only a few of which have found mention in the preceding pages, reveal Brecht as the man of the theatre he was: a brilliant innovator, a fertile mind, an iconoclast, a man with innumerable facets, but still a dramatist more capable of momentary effects than integrated wholes.

REFERENCES

1. Esslin, p. 247.
2. H. Johst, *Der Einsame*, Munich 1925, p. 6.
3. *Op. cit.*, p. 75.
4. *S.*, I, pp. 98–9.
5. Schumacher, p. 32.
6. Quoted by Schumacher, pp. 61–2.
7. *S.*, I, p. 8.
8. *S.*, II, pp. 229–30.
9. *Loc. cit.*
10. Lüthy, p. 39 and Benjamin, p. 165.
11. *Eighteenth-century Plays*, Everyman's Library, p. xii.
12. *S.*, III, p. 146.
13. *S.*, III, p. 137.
14. *S.*, III, pp. 10–11.
15. *S.*, III, p. 100., tr. from *P.* p. 153.
16. *S.*, III, p. 140, tr. from *P.* p. 177.
17. *Loc. cit.*
18. *S.*, III, p. 141.
19. Lüthy, p. 45, and Esslin, p. 206.
20. *S.*, IV, p. 302.
21. *Loc. cit.*
22. *S.*, IV, pp. 205–6.
23. *T.*, pp. 150–2.

CHAPTER IV

THEORIES AND IMPLICATIONS

By the time he had turned to writing propagandist plays, Brecht had already begun to formulate the theoretical views concerning a "non-Aristotelian" dramaturgy, which have as often as not hindered rather than helped the appreciation of his work. The difficulties have arisen, as will be seen, from the contradictory theories expressed by Brecht at different periods of his life: like his plays, his theory changed considerably in exile. The idea eventually termed "*Verfremdung*," however, retains a constant sense throughout, for all that it is difficult to translate. It has been translated both as "estrangement," which is its original meaning in German, and as "alienation." Yet in Brecht's usage it means fundamentally no more than "making strange": "an estranging image is one which allows the object to be recognised but at the same time makes it seem strange."[1] In itself, this would scarcely imply more than the shock of recognition that art has provided always; Brecht, however, adds that once the world is presented as strange, it must also arouse in the spectator the desire to alter it. His "epic" theatre thus becomes the implement of Communism, since he takes it for granted that the way in which spectators will want to see the world altered is the Communist way.

Estrangement in this sense is not, however, an inevitable corollary of a Marxist outlook; indeed the theory has so far made little progress in Communist countries, and in the Soviet Union none at all. To understand more fully how Brecht came to be attached to his theory, it is worth while to take a brief look at the circumstances out of which it arose. Of the producers who dominated the stage in Brecht's early manhood, two, Reinhardt and Piscator, laid a special emphasis on the participation of the audience in events on stage. Reinhardt, in Vienna, was known for the mysterious, enchanted atmospheres he was able to evoke, as well as for his devices for bridging the gap between audience and actors: he planted rostra deep into the auditorium, scattered actors among the seats; in a famous production of a miracle play he gave the impression that all were united in a single action. "The scene became a cathedral," wrote a contemporary observer, "and we were imprisoned in the aisles, spectators on the stage itself."[2] Piscator, meanwhile, in Berlin, though his aims were entirely different, achieved similar effects. From him Brecht learned several of the devices which later came to be associated with his own productions, notably the use of films or projected photographs as background to the stage action, and the use of a moving belt to allow characters to walk continuously without changing their position on stage. Piscator's purpose was, however, to make a performance at the theatre into one united demonstration of working-class solidarity. Proletarian organisations were the audience, proletarians the actors, and all were to be welded together in a realisation of their common cause.[3] In the view of some critics, however, the main argument against Piscator's theatre was that it substituted an emotional and imagined unity, derived from art, for a real unity in the world outside the theatre. The workers tended to be satisfied with a purely theatrical effect, and were left with no stronger resolve to establish working-class unity in the real world.

It was against this conception of the theatre, as much as against the "bourgeois" conception of Reinhardt, that Brecht's statement of principles rather arbitrarily arose. Arbitrarily, because the theatre can equally well operate after the fashion of a ritual, strengthening and sustaining faith, as after the fashion of a debate: both possibilities, without exhausting the theatre's functions, have their peculiar excellences. Brecht himself was to take a similar view later on. For the time being, he aimed at a theatre in which there should be no possibility of connexion between spectator and stage. In the past, he believed, a view of the drama which he called Aristotelian had prevailed, according to which the spectator was purged of fear and pity, and rendered a harmless member of socicty whose feelings were used up in the witnessing of purely theatrical events.[4] (This view of Aristotle is not the only possible interpretation of his theories; for a different one, Humphry House's *Aristotle's Poetics* may be consulted.)[5] In the future, a non-Aristotelian or "epic" theatre needed to be created, and its qualities were brought out in the rather over-schematised formula written by Brecht in 1931:

Dramatic Form of the Theatre	*Epic Form of the Theatre*
active	narrative
involves the spectator in a stage-action	makes the spectator an observer, but
consumes his capacity to act	awakens his capacity to act
allows him to have feelings	demands decisions from him
experience	view of the world
spectator drawn into something	he is confronted with something
suggestion	argument
feelings are preserved	feelings driven into becoming realisations
the spectator stands inside, experiences with the characters	the spectator confronts and studies what he sees
man is assumed to be known	man is an object of investigation
man unalterable	man alterable and altering

suspense in awaiting the outcome	suspense at the process
one scene exists for another	each scene for itself
growth	montage
linear progress	in curves
evolutionary inevitability	sudden leaps
man as fixed	man as a process
thought determines Being	social Being determines thought
feeling	reason[6]

As Brecht observed, these are not absolute opposites, rather a matter of emphases.[7] However, he gave the impression at the time, a justified one in view of his propagandist plays, that he discountenanced all emotion, and was obliged to correct this explicitly at a later stage.[8] Again, it is not possible to see how complete detachment can give the impetus to action: only by being "involved" in some way can the spectator gain the emotional force necessary to make his reaction more than the working-out of a syllogism. Some of Brecht's items are obscure: there is no telling what he means when he says that in the "dramatic" form man is assumed to be known. No dramatist who matters ever assumed that. Nor is man generally supposed to be unalterable: dramatists have depicted a wide variety of developments of character reaching as far as superlative wisdom. What Brecht had in mind here, however, was the tragic outcome of so many plays: this, which he regarded as fatalism, he refused to accept.[9] Man must be shown as capable of avoiding tragedy.

With this much "*Verfremdung*" of Brecht's own list, it is useful to turn now to the means whereby he sought to encourage audiences to adopt the attitudes indicated in the right-hand column. He often required very strong illumination of the stage throughout, even in night-time scenes, to avoid giving the spectator any opportunity of sinking into reverie or of feeling himself linked in the darkness with those around him.[10] Similarly, in early days he required the spotlights and floods to be actually visible on stage. "Nobody would expect the lights to be hidden at a sporting event, for instance a boxing match. However much the presentations of the new theatre may differ from sporting ones, they do not differ on the point where the old theatre finds it necessary to hide the sources of light."[11] In fact, Brecht did not adopt this practice with the Berliner Ensemble, just as he withdrew from sight the gramophone which produced sound-effects, when he found it merely aroused amusement. Further, the action was commented upon or announced by intervening or accompanying projections, a practice which Brecht continued in all his productions, although it has been felt at times to be an affectation.[12] At the Berlin production of *A Man's a Man* the figures of the actors were projected on to large boards during the performance.[13] The British soldiers in the same play appeared as enormous figures with padded chests, hideous faces, and walking on stilts. Those in *Edward II* had their faces made up completely white, to indicate—or rather to make the audience suddenly grasp at—the fear with which they entered the battle. Something of this grotesqueness remained even in the later productions, especially in the masks with protruding eyeballs worn by the soldiers in *The Caucasian Chalk Circle*. On the whole, however, the later productions forewent many of the more surprising features of the earlier practice. In the twenties, Brecht was still concerned to avoid anything beautiful, lyrical, or directly moving. He denied emotion, as he denied beauty, as an indulgence that could not be afforded while suffering still existed elsewhere. Only rational thought would serve to change the human situation as he saw it.

Estrangement was not, however, merely a matter of production technique. The style of acting also required a radical change. Brecht conceived the bourgeois actor as giving himself up to his part completely (a view which has been strongly denied),[14] so that the highest praise he might wish to hear would be, "He didn't merely *act* Lear; he *was* Lear." Brecht required his actors to maintain the same distance from the characters they were portraying as the audience was expected to adopt. "He has merely to show the character, or better, not merely to experience it; but this does not mean that when he has to act passionate people he himself must remain cold. It is only that his feelings should not be fundamentally the same as those of his character, so that the feelings of his audience do not become fundamentally those of his character. The audience must have complete liberty here."[15] The basic function of the actor is thus to "show," just as a person in conversation may break off in order to demonstrate in pantomime a part of his story. (In a provocative image, Brecht sought to stress this point by recommending to the actor the attitude of a man who puts aside his cigarette for a moment in order to act out the scene he is describing.) The methods by which this attitude was inculcated were numerous. Actors were encouraged at rehearsals to translate their speeches into the third person, preceding them with the words "He said," or to describe their actions in the past tense as they performed them. They spoke the stage instructions, indicating mood or gesture, along with their own words, and exchanged parts with one another. Brecht wrote "practice-texts" to be used at rehearsals, especially those of plays from the classic repertory. In one of these, intended for rehearsals of *Macbeth*, the porter's wife lays the blame for a theft of her own on another person, in much the same way as Lady Macbeth "gilds the faces of the grooms" to plant guilt on them for her own murder of Duncan. The actress who plays both these parts at rehearsals is unlikely to have any illusions left about the tragic grandeur of the heroine she portrays.[16]

The effect of such acting can be seen in the war-dance

of Mother Courage's son Eilif, as performed by the outstanding actor Ekkehard Schall. The exultant savagery here is at once brutal and restrained. The dancer leaps high in the air, his sabre clasped between both hands above his head; but the head leans to one side, and the lips are pursed as though in an effort to recall the next movement. Eilif is "shown" here as a young man who dances the war-dance because he believes it the right thing to do, but who is not wholly at home in it. The denial of a part of his humanity becomes evident, and the contemporary relevance of the action dawns through.

The application of Brecht's theory to production and acting techniques, though important, should not conceal the fact that the "estrangement" effect is written into the structure and language of the plays themselves. A frequent structural device is the repetition or duplication of characters or events. Herr Puntila in his drunken, generous mood comments implicitly on Herr Puntila in his sober intolerance. The "good woman" Shen Te assumes a mask of harsh oppressiveness and turns into the businessman Shui Ta, so that each of her twin personalities recalls the possibility of the other: neither is fixed and unalterable. *He who said No* repeats almost identically the plot and situations of *He who said Yes* (much as the second act of Beckett's *Waiting for Godot* repeats the first act—a surely not fortuitous coincidence); seeing much the same events enacted a second time, the audience can afford to sit back and think, rather than allow itself to be carried away by the action. Even in so early a play as *Drums in the Night* Brecht employs a similar device: an argument is in progress at a restaurant when a new diner arrives, and the waiter rehearses to him all the steps in the argument as it has progressed so far. Once again the repetition serves as an occasion for critical withdrawal. Similarly, in *The Exception and the Rule* the events which the audience has just seen on stage are summarised and partly re-enacted in the trial at the end. Indeed, the trial-scene, which affords obvious possibilities of vividly presenting occurrences which are no longer actually happening (are "in the past tense," happening to other people, as in Brecht's rehearsal methods) is one of his most often-used devices. Equally distancing is the scene in *The Mother* where the workers explain to the audience how they acted in a recent demonstration at which they came into conflict with the authorities, and go through the motions once again. Brecht purposely does not supply a scene portraying the demonstration itself, but encourages the audience to look back upon it as the characters themselves are doing. Much the same effect is achieved in *The Measures Taken*, where the agitators preface each scene as they narrate it to the chorus with the words "We will show you how it was," and in *The Good Woman of Setzuan*, where Mrs Yang steps out of her part to tell the audience of a past event which is then enacted in her presence.

Different, yet similar in effect, is the scene in *Herr Puntila*, where the chauffeur Matti pretends to make love to Puntila's daughter in order to provoke her fiancé, the diplomatic attaché. Here the action is entirely in the present. Matti goes through the motions of making improper suggestions, while it is perfectly clear that he does not mean them seriously, and since neither character is properly in his role, the audience once again is able to watch with detachment. In the same play, Puntila's daughter looks forward to the future when she will be Matti's wife, and tries to act out the situation of a working-class woman welcoming her husband home from work. With her wealthy background, she makes blunder after blunder, while each correction from Matti brings out the discrepancy between the harder life of a poor woman and her own. Thus a world of poverty which is never directly presented is conjured up by reaction from the events in the play itself.

Brecht frequently abandons the complexities of exposition in his plays. Characters do not sustain the illusion that they are unaware of the audience's presence and must reveal themselves and their relationships by carefully-dropped hints which must still preserve the appearance of being natural ingredients of their conversation. In *The Mother*, Pelagea Vlassova begins the play by directly addressing the audience, explaining who she is, and what her problems are. The same simple opening is found in *The Threepenny Opera* and *The Good Woman of Setzuan*. Alternatively, the audience is placed in possession of the necessary facts of the situation by a narrator who sits at one side of the stage throughout, as in *The Caucasian Chalk Circle*. And in most of the plays the action is interrupted by songs which summarise, comment on, or predict the action. In all these ways it becomes inevitable that whatever method of acting or production is used, some element of estrangement will make itself felt.

In its widest sense, however, Brecht claimed, estrangement is not a matter of special techniques, but a bringing-to-consciousness of a normal procedure of everyday life. "The estrangement effect," he wrote, "occurs when the thing to be understood, the thing to which attention is to be drawn, is changed from an ordinary, well-known, immediately present thing into a particular, striking, unexpected thing. In a certain sense the self-evident is made incomprehensible, although this only happens in order to make it all the more comprehensible."[17] This, he adds, is a matter of everyday occurrences. A man realises more vividly that his mother is the wife of another man when he becomes a stepson. A car is estranged when we have been used to driving a modern one and suddenly find ourselves driving a Ford model T. We hear explosions again and realise that the engine is a combustion engine: we begin to be surprised that a vehicle can be drawn along without horses, "in short, we comprehend the car by conceiving it as something strange, new, as a successful construction, and thereby to some extent as something unnatural."[18] Any device which introduces this strangeness produces an estrangement to some degree, even such simple words as "actually" and "really," whereby we seek to impress our hearers more vividly with what we are saying.

As Reinhold Grimm has pointed out, this means that almost every linguistic device used by Brecht can be reckoned among his estrangement effects. The essential feature is that there should be some contrast: the spectator's mind is brought to dwell on the opposite of what is said or performed, or two versions of an event are given simultaneously, or a comparison is implied. The result is always that attention is drawn to other possibilities, while it is affirmed that only the one, particular possibility has taken shape. Thus, to quote Grimm, the proclamation by the judge in *Round Heads and Pointed Heads* is estranging, when he announces: "In the case of the Barefooted Beggar-Monks of San Stefano against the Needy Sisters of San Barabas, the claim for damages by the Barefooted Beggar-Monks is assessed at seven million." Or again, the highwayman Macheath in *The Threepenny Opera* declares that "between ourselves, it's only a matter of weeks before I go over into banking completely." Similarly, Simone Machard, the modern Joan of Arc, is told by her supposed ecclesiastical judges, "you will be handed over to a higher court which will decide why you are to be condemned to death at the stake."[19] In each case, something surprising is announced in a matter-of-fact tone of voice, and the spectator is expected to feel this surprise and react accordingly. Yet, as Grimm's examples show, the effect need not be as liberating for the spectator as the theory might lead one to suppose. It can limit him to a single reaction, the mere reverse of what he hears affirmed, without necessarily stimulating him to original thinking.

In fact, when the meaning of estrangement is extended as widely as it is by Grimm, to cover parodistic quotation, metaphor, puns, and other common techniques, it begins to lose all specific meaning, and can be applied to very many of the normal devices of literary composition. There is a difference between making a scene come alive (or making its opposite come alive in the spectator's mind) and encouraging the spectator to bring about a change in the world as he finds it. This difference corresponds to a difference between Brecht's conception of estrangement when he first began to expound it explicitly, in the early thirties, and his conception of it in the forties and fifties. In the earlier days, his purpose had been primarily political: he had intended to "turn a means of enjoyment into a lesson to be taught, and to transform certain institutions [*sc.* the theatres] from places of entertainment into organs of publicity."[20] His plays at that time had largely followed that precept: the estrangement in *The Measures Taken*, for instance, is achieved partly by the workers on stage who personify the "right" attitude to the events they are witnessing. To quote a Communist critic, Brecht employed a didacticism, at that time, "which only allowed such associations as the poet intended."[21] The events on stage are thus certainly made to look strange, but do not necessarily bring a sense of vividness or surprise. They bring the mind of the spectator to a particular train of thought (against which he may well react) but do not give him that sense of a pristine reality which may be gained through the devices of poetry and art in general. The difference is that between an estrangement effect which leads to a single political response, and thereby to action, and an effect which leads to an aesthetic realisation, to wonder, awe, contemplation, exhilaration, or grief. In contrast to the propagandist works, the later plays allow for more scope for this kind of effect, and at the same time their political message becomes much less incisive.

This difference becomes the more marked when one turns to Brecht's later theoretical writings. In the *Little Organon for the Theatre*,[22] written in 1948, he deliberately recalls his earlier writings only in order to reject them:

at that time, he says, he had "threatened to 'turn a means of enjoyment into a lesson to be taught, and transform certain institutions from places of entertainment into organs of publicity,' i.e. to emigrate from the realms of pleasure. . . . Let us now, no doubt to the general regret, recant our intention to emigrate from the realms of pleasure and announce, no doubt to even more general regret, our intention of settling in those realms. Let us treat the theatre as a place of entertainment, as a true aesthetics should, and let us find out what sort of entertainment appeals to us."[23] The theatre was to be neither moralising nor didactic; it was merely to detach itself from the classical models that had suited former ages, and produce entertainment adapted to our own age. In other words, it was to be a theatre scientific in mood, which was as much as to say, in Brecht's eyes, one that was Communistic in mood, since Communism represented for him the scientific way of looking at the universe. At this point in his manifesto, however, Brecht ran into a certain amount of self-contradiction. On the one hand, he continued to emphasise the function of the theatre as a contribution to the political struggle—and the turgidity of his language, often found in his explicitly Marxist writings, is significant in itself: "We need a theatre which does not merely make possible the emotions, insights and impulses allowed by the relevant field of human relationships in which the actions occur, but one which utilizes and produces thoughts and feelings which themselves play a part in altering the field."[24] Here, Brecht is clearly thinking of the estrangement effect in terms of his propagandist plays of the early thirties. Towards the end of the same essay, however, he adopts a different standpoint, more in harmony with the spirit of much of his later work. In words that recall his own partly sympathetic treatment of the capitalist Puntila he writes: "Society can derive enjoyment even from the asocial, so long as it displays vitality and greatness . . . Even a river that has catastrophically broken loose can freely be enjoyed by society in all its glory if society is able to master it: for then it belongs to society."[25] Here already there are signs of an aesthetic attitude—for all that the "asocial" is to be mastered, its qualities are appreciated. This tendency becomes even more apparent later on. It is not a question of portraying successes or failures, Brecht continues: all attempts at refashioning society (not merely Communist attempts, apparently), whether they are shown in literature to have failed or succeeded, give us "a feeling of triumph and confidence and provide us with pleasure at the possibilities of change in all things. Galileo expresses this [in Brecht's play] when he says 'It is my opinion that the world is a very noble and admirable place, in view of all the different changes and generations that constantly occur in it'."[26] The criterion here is not the good of society, nor is the ultimate aim the classless society: rather, in either contemplative or enthusiastic fashion, change is welcomed for its own sake, and the highest pleasure is the morally-unmoved witnessing of such change. The nature of the change scarcely seems to matter here. Whereas in the propagandist plays Brecht had intended to alter the structure of society for the benefit of the under-privileged, he now welcomes the sheer dynamism of the flux of life. With this conception, the effect of estrangement is altered. It does not teach a lesson, or at least not a political one. If anything is to be derived from the theatre it is derivable by the individual rather than by society, and in terms of pleasure rather than profit. "It [the theatre] should not even be expected to teach, at all events nothing more useful than how to conduct oneself pleasurably, whether in a physical or an intellectual sense."[27] The role of the theatre is to be something "entirely superfluous," and the purpose of living is to enjoy this superfluity above all else. Indeed, there is nothing comparable to the pleasure to be derived from artistic presentations. At the play, the worker can survey at a distance the kaleidoscopic changes of life, and the ideal of a purpose underlying these changes is apparently to be abandoned. "Let him [the worker] in his theatre enjoy as an entertainment the terrible and never-ending labours which serve to sustain him, together with the terrors of his ceaseless transformation. Here let him produce himself in the easiest way, for the easiest form of existence is in art."[28] Clearly, if a spectator is enjoying the representation of terrors, even in an extended use of the word "enjoy," he is by so much the less preparing to alter them, and by so much the more accepting the prospect of a continual change that has no ultimate purpose. In these last words of the *Organon* Brecht reverts to an attitude akin to that he had expressed through *Baal*: the all-accepting, amoral delight in the dreadful as well as in the more obviously pleasurable consequences of being alive.

Brecht is, however, not exactly anti- or un-Marxist here. A similar, in fact a rhapsodic enjoyment of the "eternal cycle" of matter is equally to be found in the principal exponents of Marxist philosophy. "We have the certainty," writes Engels, "that matter remains eternally the same in all its transformations, that none of its attributes can ever be lost, and therefore, also, that with the same iron necessity with which it will again exterminate on the earth its highest creation, the thinking mind, it must somewhere else and at another time again engender it."[29] This Heraclitan welcome to the changing world, with its strange parallel in the Nietzschean doctrine of Eternal Recurrence, is paradoxically as much a part of Marxism as its eschatological vision of a classless society. Brecht does no more here than pursue the paradoxes of his masters.

The later theory, then, while it still includes a political purpose, combines with it an aesthetic attitude which it makes no attempt to reconcile with the other. Of the two trends, moreover, the aesthetic one is given much the greater emphasis, so that it is not surprising to find, in many of the later plays, a merely ostensible Communist solution to the social problems set forth. Brecht's aesthetics reveal their weakest point, however, in their complete irrelevance to tragedy, their insistence that the tragedies of the past as presented by Shakespeare and Sophocles are now to be presented as avoidable. It is all very well to speak of catastrophes being enjoyed by society in all their glory, so long as they remain potential catastrophes under society's control. Yet human history is full of catastrophes, individual and national, which could not be controlled, and tragedy has relentlessly confronted these, grasping at the worst and enduring it without pessimism or resignation. For this form of drama Brecht has no place. In theory at least, his men and women are either the misguided sufferers of the past, from whom a lesson can be drawn, or the exultant revellers in the contradictions of the present moment. For the millions who even in recent years have seen final and inevitable disaster threaten, disaster which, when it came, could only be met in the spirit and in faith, Brecht has no word to offer. Yet in one play, at least, he achieved tragic effects which outweigh the inconsistencies of his theory.

REFERENCES

1. *S.T.*, p. 150.
2. E. Stern and H. Herald, *Reinhardt und seine Bühne*, Berlin 1919, p. 106.
3. E. Piscator, *Das politische Theater*, 1929.
4. Cp. Nietzsche, *Menschliches, Allzumenschliches*, I, para. 148.
5. See also G. Zwerenz, *Aristotelische und Brechtsche Dramatik*.
6. *S.*, III, pp. 266–7.
7. *Loc. cit.*
8. *T.*, p. 244.
9. *V.*, 12, p. 121.
10. *V.*, 11, p. 97.
11. *Loc. cit.*

12. Willett, in *Adam and Encore* article.
13. *V.*, 11, p. 99.
14. Michael Redgrave and Jean-Louis Barrault, in *World Theatre*, IV, 1, pp. 30–6.
15. *V.*, 12, p. 127.
16. *V.*, 11, p. 109.
17. *V.*, 11, p. 102.
18. *V.*, 11, p. 103.
19. Grimm, p. 27.
20. *S.*, III, p. 276.
21. *S.F.*, 2, p. 357.
22. *V.*, 12, pp. 107–40.
23. *V.*, 12, pp. 109–10.
24. *V.*, 12, p. 122.
25. *V.*, 12, p. 119.
26. *V.*, 12, p. 137.
27. *V.*, 12, p. 111.
28. *V.*, 12, p. 140.
29. Karl Marx and Friedrich Engels, *Selected Works*, Moscow 1958, VOL. II, p. 79.

CHAPTER V

LATER PLAYS

Brecht's earlier plays show a curious development. *Baal* had been an extraordinarily impressive work, brutal, coarse, tender, delighted, and, as Herbert Lüthy has said, "not morbid at all. . . . It is really careless, joyous and with genuine spiritual depth. What is presented here in the language of decomposition is the life-process itself, the great orgiastic metamorphosis of nature."[1] But Baal had been isolated in his enjoyment. The need to come to terms with a social reality as harsh and chaotic as any Germany has seen drove Brecht into a falsity that shows itself in the hysteria of his St Joan, and the engineered inhumanity of *The Measures Taken.* Emerging from isolation with a desperate urge to put right the social evils he saw, he fell into the trap that waits for all of us who have a moral conscience: he lost his integrity and became a fanatic. Yet the frankness which is one of the chief virtues of *Baal* still remained, and it is refreshing to see, in several of the later plays, how it was vindicated.

A beginning may be made with a work in which Brecht takes up the theme of a number of earlier plays, that of the compassionate reformer. In contrast to the propagandist works, *The Good Woman of Setzuan* (1938–41) treats this with a new complexity. In structure, this is by no means "epic" theatre: the plot is an extremely complicated affair rather than a concatenation; in addition, there is an intensity of argument, an exaggerated caricaturing of situations, which both recall the earliest plays and make it difficult to preserve an attitude of detachment, although devices of estrangement are employed. The clarity of outline in the propagandist plays has gone. Yet this lack of clarity adds to the dramatic interest. Instead of a biased message, a dialectic of opposing attitudes emerges, providing tension and involvement in the manner of the traditional theatre. At the same time, it will be seen that without some degree of detachment also the play is liable to be misunderstood.

The "argument," which is perhaps the most important element here, concerns three Chinese gods who come in search of good men, as Jehovah once came to Sodom. They find none except the prostitute Shen Te, and reward her with money which she uses to set up a shop. At once, however, she is besieged with beggars and needy friends, and her generosity is so great that she is soon on the verge of ruin. Later, she falls in love with an unemployed airman, Sun, a ruthlessly selfish man to whom she still shows complete devotion, and here again her goodness leads to disaster. In her dilemma, she sees no way out but to disguise herself as a male cousin, Shui Ta, who puts an end to the innumerable claims on her love by showing a hard insistence on principle. As Shui Ta, she helps both the poor and her lover, setting up a factory which provides work and wages; but in doing so, she foregoes almost all her charity, and her mental plight is even worse. At length, she is arrested as Shui Ta for the supposed murder of Shen Te. The gods enter the court to try the case, whereupon she reveals that she is herself Shen Te. At this, the gods are delighted, for the good woman is still on earth, but Shen Te desperately protests that she is not merely the good woman: she cannot do without her cousin. The gods, however, are unconcerned. A sparing use of Shui Ta, they suggest, say once a month, is permissible, and with this they return to heaven in pink clouds of glory, leaving Shen Te writhing in her agonies of conscience. An epilogue informs the audience that this is not a satisfactory conclusion, and urges them to think of a better one themselves.

There is a strong temptation to respond to these situations in traditional fashion, to see the play as exploring a literal interpretation of the commandment to love our neighbours, and showing the disasters attendant on such a course, as Ibsen did in *Brand* or Tolstoy in *The Light Shines in the Darkness*. On these terms, the play is tragic in that it shows the utter impossibility of human goodness. Alternatively, the thought occurs to mind of an interpretation in existentialist terms, demonstrating the absurdity of virtue but affirming it nevertheless as a human achievement poised over a void of meaninglessness, roughly as in Miller's *The Crucible* or Sartre's *The Flies*. There is much to be said for this, for Shen Te's extreme devotion, folly as it is, arouses a deep admiration. But Brecht's play is even more complex than this, and yet a third possibility needs to be borne in mind. In a foreword (omitted in the later edition), Brecht once observed that "the province Setzuan in this parable, which stood for all places where men are exploited by men, is such a place no longer."[2] In other words, this is essentially a picture of a competitive society, its problems are those of capitalism and not of modern Communist China, and with this an entirely new "distancing" attitude is gained. If an audience receives the play in the spirit advocated by Brecht, it may well feel, in part at least, not admiration for Shen Te's quixotic charity, nor oppression at her tragedy, but amazement that such ideals could ever capture a human heart. "I wouldn't have thought that.—That's not the way to do it.—That's most remarkable, scarcely believable. This has got to stop.—I am shattered by the suffering of this man, because there could be a way out for him."[3] This is the attitude Brecht expected, and it may well lead us to consider more closely the discussion between Wang the water-carrier and the three gods, in which Wang proposes that the ideals set before men should be not love but benevolence, not justice but fairness, not honour but decency, in short that almost unattainable absolutes should be replaced by more human qualities.[4] Indeed, there is a sense in which the play sets out to show that it is precisely Shen Te's devotion to an impossible ideal which transforms her into her ruthless counterpart: because she cannot love all men equally, she despairs and seeks to achieve her ends by cruelty. Love, in short, paradoxically gives rise to capitalism. A Confucian attachment to "the mean" is more human-hearted. On these terms, the moral of the parable is not so much, as John Willett suggests, "that in a competitive society goodness is often suicidal,"[5] but rather that the competitive society is a concomitant of the quest for absolute goodness.

Yet whatever Brecht may have thought, this solution still leaves problems. It has been seen how, in his own life, the desire to do good led to the deliberate injunction to "embrace the butcher," and Communism demands as much as capitalism that evil be done so that good may come. In fact a Communist critic sees the message of the play precisely in the need for determined action. Fantastically taking Shui Ta as his model, he declares that "to be good, I must be cruel,"[6] recalling that in every country Communism has been achieved only by means comparable to Shui Ta's. Benevolence, fairness, and decency do not provide the driving urge to "change the world" (a phrase which recurs several times in the play); only the impossible standards, with all their dangers, spur men on.

But after all, the play does not advocate, it presents, and one particular virtue it has is its ability to arouse a ferment of thoughts. For the Christian it brings home an unwelcome realisation. As Archbishop Temple said, "no one does accept the Christian standard for himself; that Jesus of Nazareth did so is precisely what constitutes the gulf between Him and other men."[7] Brecht, like Tolstoy and Ibsen, rubs in this frank confession till it smarts. He also brings out the "scandal" of Christianity (for all that the atmosphere is Buddhist), its affront to all accepted standards of human conduct. Love like Shen Te's is sheer folly, and Brecht does not allow us the flattering thought that it is divine "foolishness," to use St Paul's term, nevertheless. Equally, however, he cannot mean to ask for detachment alone. We are shocked at Shen Te's unreasoning devotion to her lover when he has already revealed to her, in her guise of Shui Ta, his unscrupulous intention to exploit her, and his total lack of any reciprocating love. We feel, as Brecht intended, astonished indignation at this blindness of hers. On the other hand, when she explains her motives later, it is impossible to feel only detached:

> I saw him at night, puffing out his cheeks
> in his sleep: they were evil.
> And in the morning I held his coat up to the
> light: I could see the wall through it.
> When I saw his cunning laughter I was
> afraid, but
> When I saw the holes in his shoes, I loved
> him very much.[8]

Only a complete inhumanity could find this absurd, want to change it, or claim that there is another way out. And so also in the final scene, there is a mingling of deep sympathy and surprise. This is not at all the ending of *St Joan*, where once again a rosy light shines down on a woman who is being canonised for all the "wrong" reasons. There, the one-sided intention was obvious: in the eyes of Christians, Joan was a saint; in her own eyes, enlightened by Communism, her Christian charity had been a subtle poison. Here, while the gods sing the praises of the good woman, she herself is conscious of her failure not by Communist but by charitable standards. We, the spectators, meanwhile, see Shen Te's folly and find ourselves unable to give any other name to it. We reach out for alternatives such as those suggested by Wang and find them unsatisfying too. We reach out for traditional standbys: "Suffering purifies," "courage grows with danger," "good wins in the end," and find these already stultified by the mouths of the gods. There is no way out, universal charity reveals itself as the nearly suicidal doctrine which we see it to have been in the life of the modern saint, Simone Weil. But, with all this, Brecht makes clear his thorough personal acquaintance and even his sympathy with the dilemma of Shen Te. He sees the absurdity, but unlike the existentialists he does not affirm any need for commitment to the absurd. Rather, he looks for another way out, and it is this that gives the play its completely open ending, leaving decision this time entirely in the audience's hands. It is no longer the case that only those associations are permitted which the author had in mind; instead, a real freedom is accorded.

A real freedom, however, with one limitation. In the epilogue, the audience is asked to think whether it is a new Man that is needed, a new world, new gods or perhaps none at all. It is suggested, then, that the situation of the play is relevant to the religious problems of contemporary Europe, to which answers may be found either in a new religion or in atheism. Yet the three Chinese gods do not remotely correspond to any Christian doctrines of divinity. The notion of a god who requires men to be perfectly good but provides them with no assistance ignores completely the Christian belief in the Holy Spirit, and makes of Christianity a purely moralistic religion. Christians do not believe that man is called upon to be perfect by his own efforts, rather that all good acts proceed not from man but from God. This is a belief that has its difficulties, and for two thousand years new thinkers have sought to redefine its meaning for their own generation. But in a portrayal of present-day religion it cannot simply be swept aside as Brecht does here. Our ancestors were not so naïve as all that. What Brecht has written in this play is in fact an exploration of the moral position of the deist, and its unresolved conclusion, frank as it is, belongs rather to deism than the theistic religion of traditional Christianity.

Yet with all this, the really essential quality of the play is still untouched, for the operation of the estrangement effect has unpredictable results. Picasso has explained his own policy in art in terms closely similar to Brecht's. "My landscapes," he writes, "are exactly like my nudes and my still lifes; but with faces people see the nose is crooked, whereas nothing shocks them about a bridge. But I drew this 'crooked nose' on purpose. I did what was necessary to force people to see a nose. Later on they saw—or they will see—that the nose isn't crooked at all. What I had to do was to stop them from going on seeing only 'beautiful harmonies' or 'exquisite colour'."[9] Whether Brecht has in the end done the same for moral issues in this play as Picasso did for the nose is something that can only be discovered by arguing with the play, entering into its disputes, opposing it and at the same time being ready to admit defeat. If that is done, *The Good Woman* will be found to have an explosive force which no amount of comment will reveal.

In *The Life of Galileo*, written in 1937–9, but with additions made in 1945–7, Brecht takes further the idea implicit in one aspect of *The Good Woman*—that of a possible system of ethics not based on absolute standards. As the play was first written, it is said, it had much more the look of a direct advocacy of such a system than it has in its final form.[10] In this earlier version, Galileo is shown as an old man who outwits the Inquisition, refusing to become a martyr by submitting to torture, but secretly and cunningly continuing the scientific work which the Church has condemned, and smuggling his writings abroad under the noses of the authorities. Here, then, what John Willett says, apparently of the final version, is probably true: Galileo's recantation is justified, "and so we arrive at a shifting system of social ethics, where nothing can be taken as fixed outside its context or its time."[11] Yet when we do come to the final version, there is much that speaks against this. Here, Galileo recants not from any superior cunning but from cowardice at the sight of the instruments of torture; after his recantation he conducts his investigations secretly, but half ashamedly, and holds himself unworthy to shake the hand of a fellow-scientist. His successful adaptation to circumstances proves his undoing at the crucial moment of his life. It is true that Brecht also arouses our sympathy for Galileo in this tremendous failure, and the parting words of Andrea in the next to last scene echo in the mind when the play is over: "I can't believe your murderous [self-] analysis will be the last word."[12] Nevertheless, the analysis, if not the last, is one of the words that count in this play where, as in *The Good Woman*, a dual mood reigns. Brecht is as relentless here in depicting Galileo's shifting ethics as he was in depicting Shen Te's unshakable adherence to a standard, and as he said himself, "in view of the situation one can scarcely be bent on either simply praising Galileo or simply condemning him."[13]

The difficulty about a dual attitude like this is that it tends to produce an equanimity of the kind that Brecht had always bitterly attacked. Thus the *Sunday Times*, in reviewing an English performance of *Galileo*, spoke of how difficult it was to be truly revolutionary, and suggested that Brecht was already as conventionally acceptable as Ibsen and Whistler.[14] That Brecht was aware of this difficulty is apparent from his own extremely fair-minded comments on the play, published after his death.[15] In fact he could not afford to indulge in the liking for a "synthesis"—a fusion of two opposing attitudes—which has marked German literature for almost two centuries now: he had to shock, and the positions taken up by characters in his plays had to inspire extremes of sympathy and aversion. Without that, there would always be too great a preparedness, especially in German audiences, to accept gratefully the idea that Galileo was somehow right in his wrongness or wrong in his rightness. The mental labour, fear, hope, uncertainty, faith, passion, and compassion necessary to reach a synthesis which is in the end perhaps justifiable after all, for an instant less than the beating of an artery, would never be experienced at any level of reality. For Brecht since early days had never given way to nihilism:

> He who is defeated cannot escape from
> Wisdom.
> Hold on to yourself and sink. Be afraid.
> But sink. At the bottom
> The lesson awaits you.[16]

The "lesson" at that time had been the lesson of Communism, which always remained as Brecht's sheet-anchor. But in these later plays more than a political theory was involved, and Brecht was as much concerned to arouse a sober enthusiasm as to incite to political action.

A fault of the English production of *Galileo* just referred to was that it did not shock. A Galileo who appears on stage in the first scene, as Brecht requires him to do, to expound the Ptolemaic and Copernican systems for the benefit of a small boy, is likely to look a pedagogue. His lecture takes on a different flavour when it is delivered as it was by Charles Laughton, with Brecht's approval, by a Galileo taking his morning wash, stripped to the waist. Galileo's pleasure here is not merely intellectual but physical also, in fact his appetite for knowledge has to be shown as a part of his appetite for all things. "His voluptuous way of moving about," Brecht wrote of Laughton's performance, "and the movements of his hands in his trouser-pockets when he was planning new researches, were all but scandalous. Whenever Galileo was being creative, Laughton revealed a contradictory mixture of aggressiveness and defenceless softness and sensitivity."[17] Galileo's thirst for knowledge is Gargantuan; he is a colossus, but a colossus who, in the opening scene, drinks milk. For the sake of continuing his researches he is prepared to stay in Florence during a plague, yet when a different death threatens, from the Inquisition, he yields without a fight. He will not tolerate a moment's divagation from complete honesty in his search for truth, yet he is unscrupulous in presenting to the senators of Venice as his own invention a telescope recently invented in Holland. With all this, Brecht builds up a picture of a man who would not be so creative as he is if he were not also sensuous, cowardly, tenacious, and ascetic, in short a rationalist who lives by his instincts. And thus the final scene in which Galileo appears has a strange effect of its own which yet has something in common with the other later plays. Here, Galileo has just said good-bye to his former pupil Andrea, now a grown man; Andrea is persuaded that his master's "new ethic" is the ethic of a new age in which adherence to rigid principle will be abandoned; Galileo remains on stage to make his supper off the goose which has been sent him. He wolfs it down with a greed which it perhaps takes a Laughton to show, thrusting down mouthful after mouthful in an insatiable desire for more life, more experience, more pleasure. We, meanwhile, his audience, feel at once the excitement and revulsion which so naked a display of human appetite brings, and the awareness that it is a concomitant of the new relativistic, all-embracing attitude represented by the Galileo of this play.

On the other hand, one comes away from a performance also with the sense of an absolute demand for courage. Galileo's dilemma has been seen, its causes traced, and sympathy for him aroused. But, as Brecht knew, and was to discover even more intensely later on in his own dilemma, the ability to adapt to circumstances has been far too prevalent in Central European countries for centuries past. The issue of Galileo's cowardice thus takes on a sharp contemporary edge: Galileo, the play affirms—and it does not so very much matter whether it is historically accurate, the moral is what counts—Galileo stands at the threshold of a new age, as we seem to do ourselves since 1945. If he recants, the cause of science will suffer a setback, for science depends on a relentless honesty, and cannot be associated with hypocrisy. The issue of martyrdom thus becomes acute, and Harold Hobson is partly right when he says: "The point of *Galileo* is that men do not today live in an age of reason simply because at a particular moment in the seventeenth century Galileo recanted before the Inquisition, instead of standing firm. As in one view humanity is saved by the grace and death of Christ, so, in Brecht's, by the life and disgrace of Galileo, humanity is damned. Galileo is nothing more nor less than Brecht's Antichrist. He is the God who failed us."[18] This point, ironically expressed as it is by Mr Hobson, is certainly a justifiable conclusion from the emotional climax reached in Scene 13, for all that Brecht sought to stress individual rather than vicarious responsibility. In his habitually exaggerating fashion Brecht does imply at this instant that a whole epoch of European history turns on one man's failure. And the intense sense of this evoked by the play is poles apart from the sympathy inspired by Galileo's "adaptations." The mood of the play as a whole is thus a mingling of Rabelaisian zest and a quasi-Christian recognition of the need for martyrdom, a mood which Rabelais himself may have shared when he allowed his gigantic Pantagruel to meditate on the death of the god Pan—"for he may lawfully be said in the Greek tongue to be *Pan*, since he is our *all*. For all that we are, all that we live, all that we have, all that we hope, is him, by him, from him, and in him. . . . for this most mighty Pan, our only Saviour, died near Jerusalem during the reign of Tiberius Caesar."[19]

The confrontation of these two attitudes makes good dramatic material, despite the fundamentally intellectual quality of the play, and it provides notable moments of conflict and tension. Weakness appears in the earlier scenes, in which Galileo's astronomical opponents are presented in so foolish a guise as to destroy interest in the arguments. In addition, the physical aspects of Galileo's delight in research, emphasised in Brecht's comments, appear seldom in the given action of the play; they may be brought out by actors, but the text itself gives comparatively little evidence of them. Here it becomes clear how much Brecht depended on the full theatrical effect rather than on the printed word. One further weakness, however, does not appear remediable. In his last long speech Galileo reviews the position of science as he now leaves it, crippled for centuries by his recantation. His own failure he declares, has been that he sought to accumulate knowledge for the sake of knowledge, without regard to the primary aim of science, the easing of human existence. He has pursued learning outside the framework of human needs, and left a legacy of knowledge divorced from social reality. "You may in timc discover everything there is to discover," he asserts, "and your progress will be merely a progress away from humanity. The gap between you and them may one day become so great that your cries of triumph at some new achievement will be answered by a universal cry of horror."[20] Brecht had in mind here, as we know from his comments, the dropping of the atom bombs on Hiroshima and Nagasaki, together with the new age of atomic energy which they heralded, events which he regarded as the direct outcome of science pursued in isolation from the needs of men. Galileo has failed, despite his Pan-like omnivorousness, to be completely human: he has ignored the call to martyrdom which is also a part of Pan, and he has ignored the social demands of his age. But—here the weakness emerges—his failure is asserted in a long and intricate monologue which relies entirely on verbal argument. There is no possibility of making this point come alive in terms of theatrical action, for the "people," the masses to whom Galileo looks for the complement to his humanity, have almost no part in the play. The final hint of a new totality of human nature, integrated individually and socially, thus remains a thought that may very well escape notice in the theatre, instead of a dramatically conceived "gesture" that makes its impact on eyes and mind at once. But we may perhaps have to thank for this the complexity, the magnitude, and the horror of the situation which Brecht, while still rewriting the play, had to confront in 1945. We are still a long way from synthesis.

With so much indication of the new treatment of old subject-matter it is useful to turn to a completely unproblematic play, written at about the same time (1940–1), *Herr Puntila and his Man Matti*, a work which belongs much more clearly to the "epic" category than either *Galileo* or *The Good Woman*. Whereas both of the latter develop an argument, present a problem, in which the spectator inevitably becomes involved, at least intellectually, *Puntila* is a loosely-strung sequence of scenes in which very little plot can be found, and enjoyment is to be had from the individual moments rather than the excitement of a progression. This "epic," or narrative quality (perhaps the picaresque novel gives the best idea of what Brecht understood by the term, although epics like the *Iliad* also depend on incident more than plot) is particularly marked in the scene where four women sit by the roadside to exchange stories and reminiscences. All thought of "dramatic" interest—tension, conflict, development—is set aside; the spectator has to be held by the sheer quality of the story-telling at the given instant. And this is characteristic of the manner of the play as a whole, for the total outline is of extreme simplicity.

Puntila is a Finnish landowner with the curious characteristic that when he is drunk he is overflowing with good humour, amatoriness, and generosity, whereas the moment he becomes sober he returns to a mean, calculating, money-centred, and business-like attitude. While sober, he proposes to marry his daughter Eva to a foppish attaché in the diplomatic service; when drunk, he is angry with her and demands that she should marry his chauffeur, Matti. His attitude changes a few times with his drinking bouts, until at length Matti declines to serve so irresponsible a master, and leaves. The rest is made up of incidents which provide Puntila with opportunities of displaying his prodigious energy and vitality. Into this plain tale Brecht weaves a certain amount of social criticism: Matti refuses to marry Eva because of her indignation when, in his wooing, he gives her a proletarian slap on the bottom, and he leaves Puntila because of his shabby treatment of a Communist farm-hand. In the background there are always indications of a starving peasantry and political persecution, and at times (as in Scene 8) a note of restrained denunciation of all capitalism is heard, the more powerful for being restrained. Yet the purport of the whole has not struck all spectators in the same way. Of Puntila himself, the obvious representative of capitalism in the play, it has been said, he "is a great character. . . . Very much against Brecht's own intention, Puntila steals the play."[21] This is a point of view which ignores much that Brecht put into the character, and yet one which can in a small measure be defended. On the other hand, a Communist comment suggests that sympathy for Puntila is very much a matter of the slant given in production. "Steckel," an observer writes, "played Puntila in Zürich before playing him in Berlin. In Zürich he played him almost without a mask, and most spectators had the impression of a sympathetic character with a few bad moments in a state of sobriety, which looked rather like a hangover, so that even these bad moments seemed excusable. In Berlin, learning from this experience, he chose a disgustingly shaped bald head, and made himself up to look like a roué. This time, his charm when drunk looked dangerous, and his genial approaches became those of a crocodile."[22] On this interpretation, the play will look decidedly anti-capitalist, and Puntila must become the stock cartoon figure of the hooligan hyena. When, however, Brecht speaks his own mind, it is clear that neither the Communist nor the anti-Communist critic is in the right. Writing in 1940, he said: "*Puntila* is anything but a *pièce à thèse* (*Tendenzstück*). The role of Puntila may not, therefore, be divested for one moment or in one single aspect of its natural charm; a special artistry will be necessary to present the drunken scenes poetically and delicately, with as much variation as possible, and the sober scenes as ungrotesquely and unbrutally as possible."[23] The fact is that, as with the character of Galileo, Brecht did not want Puntila to be either only praised or only condemned. It was certainly against his intention that Puntila should "steal the play," and such an interpretation reveals a certain sentimentality. Equally, he had no desire to denigrate the liveliness of his central character. Rather, as in his vigorous and highly entertaining re-interpretation of Molière's *Don Juan* (1952), he seems to have been attacking what he called a "parasitic enjoyment of life."[24]

It is this which gives its particular quality to the play. There is no puritanical carping at Puntila's enjoyment, indeed at times the very reverse. In the "Notturno" scene, where he waxes lyrical at the pleasure of urinating against a wall in the open air, the occasionally Rabelaisian mood of *Galileo* is well in evidence, and one understands better the apparently blasphemous remark of Baal's, that "the world is God's excrement."[25] This is sheer physical enjoyment for its own sake, quite unlikely to be affected by changes in the structure of society. The same is true of Puntila's affairs with the four working girls, to each of whom he engages himself with rings taken from a curtain-rod, and of the zest with which he crashes from place to place in his gigantic Studebaker. Yet there is also a certain reserve. Puntila may be having a wonderful time, and his escapades may be enjoyed by the audience, as Brecht suggested, in the spirit of the *commedia dell' arte*.[26] The figure of Matti is present, however, much like Don Juan's Sganarelle, to serve as an aid to estrangement. Matti represents always a downright, "working-class," point of view which is always sceptical about the enduring quality of Puntila's enthusiasms. Those productions in which he has been shown expressing a sympathetic admiration are clearly at a disadvantage in comparison with the Ensemble productions in which he maintains a stolid indifference that is only occasionally carried away.[27] Thus, towards the end, there is a fantastic climactic scene where Puntila, in his own library and well plied with liquor once again, piles up the chairs on the table to represent a near-by hill, which he climbs at no small risk. From the "summit" he sees the vast sweep of the Finnish countryside round about him, and Brecht takes the opportunity of indulging in a lyrical mood of admiration for nature which he normally denied himself. To withhold oneself from this pleasure is to misunderstand the purpose of estrangement—this landscape, though it exists only in Puntila's verbal evocation so far as the play is concerned, is there to be enjoyed. On the other hand, Matti is not carried away by Puntila's delight: he sits leaning forward with his hands loosely joined and a slightly rueful expression on his face. To Puntila's final rhapsody—"O Tavastland, the blessed! With its sky, its lakes, its people, and its forests. Tell me your heart leaps up when you see all that!" —Matti replies, "My heart leaps up when I see your forests, Herr Puntila."[28] And with this, the full flavour of Brecht's intention is given. The land is there to be enjoyed, and can be enjoyed within the play, while at the same time the restriction on a more complete enjoyment is indicated. In short, Brecht gives the fullest possible vent to the zest for living which paradoxically fired him at a time when the world was entering on its second war, he encourages a similar zest in his future audiences, and looks forward to a time when it will not be, broadly speaking, the privilege of a few. As in *Galileo*, the masses stand in the background, waiting to take the opportunity of sharing in the bounty of earth and human nature.

These three plays give some indication of the new spirit which entered Brecht's work in the early years of the war, and the two or three years preceding it. The doctrinaire spirit has disappeared, and its place has been taken by a tolerance and generosity which seeks to bring together the exuberance displayed in *Baal*, the charitableness denied in some of the propagandist plays, and the Communistic programme explicitly adopted by Brecht since the early thirties. That the last-named is least well integrated is obvious enough. Brecht no longer argues the Communist case, or even appears to argue it; he takes it for granted, feeling perhaps that his propagandist works have done all that was necessary in that direction. Dramatically speaking, meanwhile, the same tolerance and generosity yields a new kind of interest. There is no longer the tightly-knit structure and clear message of such a play as *The Measures Taken*; problems remain unsolved, or their solution is hinted at for some future date, and the audience's attention is held much more by individual scenes than by the thread of argument or plot. Nothing is fixed and determinate: despite Brecht's theoretical pronouncements there are scenes of genuine dramatic intensity, while there are also slowings of pace which allow an "epic," or indeed in some cases a lyrical, style to emerge. With this greater freedom and greater ease, the plays have both an increased clarity and a wider application, which renders them less limited in time and space and more capable of speaking to human nature regardless of class or country. (Purely propagandistic works have presumably spent their force when the aim they propagated has been achieved.) Within this small compass, however, a great deal that needs to be said has to remain on the level of generalities. The final chapter, in giving a little more space to two plays only, will attempt to show Brecht's achievement in slightly greater detail.

REFERENCES

1. Lüthy, p. 36.
2. *V.*, 12, p. 6.
3. *S.T.*, p. 63 f.
4. *S.*, VIII, p. 360.
5. Willett, p. 82.
6. *S.F.*, 2, p. 212.
7. A. E. Baker, *William Temple and His Message*, Penguin Books 1946, p. 216.
8. *S.*, VIII, pp. 343–4.
9. *The Observer*, 10 July 1960.
10. Rohrmoser, p. 403.
11. Willett, p. 81.
12. *S.*, VIII, p. 188.
13. *S.*, VIII, p. 205.
14. *Sunday Times*, 19 June 1960.
15. *S.*, VIII, pp. 196–213.
16. *V.*, 1–4, pp. 40–1.
17. *S.*, VIII, p. 210.
18. *Sunday Times*, 19 June 1960.
19. Rabelais, *Pantagruel*, IV, ch. xxviii.
20. *S.*, VIII, pp. 186–7.
21. Esslin, p. 269.
22. *T.*, p. 22.
23. *V.*, 10, p. 122.
24. *S.*, XII, p. 190.
25. *S.*, I, p. 80.
26. *V.*, 10, p. 122.
27. Photographs in *T.*, pp. 290–291.
28. *S.*, IX, p. 163.

CHAPTER VI

LATER PLAYS (continued)

The climax of Brecht's career as a dramatist, as distinct from a man of the theatre, seems to have arisen roughly between the years 1937 and 1944, and this chapter will be mainly concerned with two other plays written at that time. Also belonging to this period are the radio-play *The Trial of Lucullus* (1939) (developed later as the opera *The Condemnation of Lucullus*, see p. 16 above), a straightforward condemnation of imperialistic warfare which is strangely platitudinous in effect, and *The Resistible Ascent of Arturo Ui* (1941), a comic allegory of Hitler's rise to power in terms of the life of the gangster Al Capone. The latter, like *Schweik in the Second World War* (1941–4), which confronts Hitler himself with one of Brecht's favourite "alter egos," reveals an odd flippancy of treatment. It has some of the humour, and none of the sentimentality, of Chaplin's similar allegory, *The Great Dictator*, and yet shows no sign of the deep personal concern of Chaplin's film. Brecht's aversion to tragedy seems to have led him here into a degree of banality, for all that Ekkehard Schall's interpretation of the Ui-Capone-Hitler role at the Paris International Festival of 1960 suggested the need for a review of critical opinion. On the other hand, *The Visions of Simone Machard* (1941–3), the only other play to have been completed during the war (except *The Caucasian Chalk Circle*, to be discussed later), is an unambiguous call for heroic endeavour, inspired both by the legend of Joan of Arc and by the French Resistance movement.

Of the post-war plays little need be said here. Brecht

was soon occupied with the work of the Berliner Ensemble, bringing to theatrical life the work of his exile and creating a repertory of older plays by Hauptmann, Gorki, and others. Almost all his dramatic creativity (so far as can be seen today) went into the adaptation of earlier authors. His version of the *Antigone* of Sophocles (1947), based on the translation by Hölderlin, deliberately avoids the tragic, and by destroying all possible sympathy for King Creon turns him into a flatly rapacious caricature of Hitler. Something similar is done for *Coriolanus* (1952–3), where once again the traces of nobility, in the most unlikable of all Shakespeare's heroes, are erased to leave only the lineaments of the bloody warmonger. (Nevertheless, if Brecht's account of the hero-worshipping line normally taken by German producers is correct,[1] his version has its uses.) Only in *The Days of the Commune* (1948–9), written in reply to the Norwegian Nordahl Grieg's play on the same topic, *The Defeat*, did Brecht create afresh, and the moral here remains ambiguous: whether the Parisian Communards of 1871 were mistaken in their tactics, premature in their rising, or bent on an impossible task, is a problem that the play leaves unsolved, though one has the impression that Brecht may not have thought so. The remaining plays are all adaptations. *The Tutor* (1950), from the late eighteenth-century play by Reinhold Lenz, reinterprets the social criticism of the *Sturm und Drang* age; *The Trial of Joan of Arc* (1952) (the third play involving this heroine) is almost a "documentary," based on contemporary records—taken from a radio-play by Anna Seghers, it is difficult to see Brecht's hand in it at all. Undoubtedly the best of all these postwar works is the version of Molière's *Don Juan* (1952) already referred to—a lively satire on wealthy epicureanism which makes a notable contribution to the repertory of the German theatre. Yet in the last work of all—to an unstated extent the fruit of collaboration—Brecht appears to have succumbed once more to the propagandistic strain. *Drums and Trumpets* (1955), based on Farquhar's Restoration comedy *The Recruiting Officer*, is a tedious satire on a British colonial system which ceased to exist in this form many decades ago, if it ever existed at all. The fact that it was written is a portent of what might have become of Brecht's dramatic talent had he lived to old age in the atmosphere of the Democratic Republic.

It is pleasing, then, as well as sad, to go back to one of the earliest plays of Brecht's climactic, the chronicle of the Thirty Years' War *Mother Courage and her Children* (1938–9). This is decidedly one of the best things Brecht wrote, and it is significant of it, as an example of "epic" theatre, that it is not the story which remains most strongly in the mind, but a series of isolated moments. Mother Courage, a canteen-woman who makes a living at one remove from the war by selling food, drink, and equipment to the soldiers involved in it, is bereft of her grown-up children one after another. She flirts with a Dutch cook, takes a refugee army chaplain under her wing, but is abandoned even by these at the end, and is left to drag her covered wagon alone, while the war continues into grey infinity. As in *Puntila*, the interest is sustained, however, by the detailed working-over of individual scenes. One remembers such occasions as that in which the plump Swisscheese sits sunning himself on the step of his mother's wagon, though the text here gives no more than the line "Not many more days now when you can sit in the sun in your shirtsleeves." The sun—or rather the floods and spots and battens, for Brecht made no attempt at naturalism and the light felt purely white and electric—beat down with an intense warmth, and in the long silence which followed the spoken line a sense of pleasure at it was curiously evoked in the mind. The dramatic irony in the words was soon, however, to become apparent, for within a few moments Swisscheese was hauled off to execution by an enemy patrol, and in recollection the warm sunlight was felt to have been merciless as well as warm. And in this simple effect of stage-lighting, apparently achieved in a typically Brechtian and exaggerated way by setting all dimmers at full, there was contained, moreover, an essential mood of the play as a whole. For this dual aspect of the beneficent yet ensnaring sunlight was a reflexion of the duality running through every scene and in all the major themes. Despite the catastrophic ending, in which Mother Courage dragged her wagon round the stage to the accompaniment of a sardonic chorus from the wings, there were moments of affirmation as well. Equally as prominent in memory as that final scene was the earlier one (Scene 5) in which a chaotic panorama of human motives was presented in the ruins of a destroyed village: Mother Courage refusing to sell schnapps on credit, the chaplain burrowing in the shell of a farmhouse to save the trapped occupants, Mother Courage again refusing to give up her officers' shirts to make bandages, a soldier making off, while she argued, with a whole bottle of liquor, unobserved— and finally the dumb daughter Kattrin holding up a living baby in her arms as the curtains closed: an instant of triumphant compassion which could not abolish, and yet stood out against, the greed, malice, and uncharitableness on every hand.

The play exists in virtue of such scenes as these, and a fuller appreciation of this aspect could only multiply examples. One is struck also, however, from the outset by the extraordinary language used by all the peasant characters and military rank-and-file. It is not at all the case that *Mother Courage* is "written in the forceful, coarse language of its period";[2] Brecht had no taste for naturalistic historicism. He has, however, created a language which recaptures the vigour of Luther's German while at the same time suggesting both a Bavarian dialect form and an extremely modern economy and directness of diction. It is difficult to convey this achievement to English readers who have no German, since a part of this directness derives from English idiom. When Mother Courage observes that "Auf was ich aus bin, ist, mich und meine Kinder durchbringen mit meinem Wagen,"[3] it sounds very much as though Brecht were translating the loosely-bound phrase, "What I'm out after is to get me and my children through with the wagon," but the syntax is much more shocking in the stricter context of German. (Brecht enjoyed this anglicisation often: in *Galileo* he takes an obvious pleasure in allowing a character to repeat the terse phrase "Das ist ein Fakt," rather than the accepted German "Das ist eine Tatsache," whose rhythm is more mellifluous and "feminine.") Again, the strictly German passages often have the ring of peasant earthiness and yet are unmistakably Brechtian, as in a passage like this:

DER FELDHAUPTMANN: Ich wett, dein Vater war ein Soldat.

EILIF: Ein grosser, hör ich. Meine Mutter hat mich gewarnt deshalb. Da kann ich ein Lied.

DER FELDHAUPTMANN: Sings uns! [*Brüllend*]. Wirds bald mit dem Essen![4]

As Mennemeier says, this is "apparently realistic dialogue which in fact works with subtle abbreviations and is 'popular' only *idealiter*."[5] And to quote him again, "*Mother Courage* shows very clearly that Brecht's drastic yet intimate popular style seeks to imitate less the reality than the 'idea' of natural speech, and its typically alogical structure. The whole drama is, so far as popular usage is concerned, estranged."[6] Thus it is never possible to accept the characters on stage as figures from everyday or historical life: they are constantly bordering on reality in their speech and as constantly veering away from it with a vigour and crudity that has not yet re-entered the German language as a whole.

Despite the looseness of structure both in language and in total form, however (Mother Courage's sentence reflects linguistically the attitude which created this rambling yet forceful play), there is a binding element in the themes which run through from scene to scene. At its simplest level, *Mother Courage* is an anti-war play, denouncing the stupidity of its central characters who live by the war and yet are blind to the penalties it brings. So important was this to Brecht that, when he found his "bourgeois" audiences at the first performances in Zürich sympathising with Mother Courage, admiring her tenacity in the face of adversity, he rewrote or modified several passages, supplying baser motives for her actions and emphasising, as he did later for Coriolanus, her inhumanity. Even so, a Communist critic could still find it in him to speak of her in the revised version as "a humanist saint from the tribe of Niobe and the *mater dolorosa*, who defends the life to which she has given birth with her bared teeth and claws."[7] And it continues to be possible for critics to speak of Brecht's characters "belying his intentions,"[8] as though his deliberate alterations and emphases could be disregarded. A more accurate interpretation is likely to be that, as with Galileo and Puntila, Brecht did not intend Mother Courage to be either only praised or only condemned. There is no extant saying of his to that effect in this case, and anyhow the charge against Mother Courage should not be lightened through equivocation. As with Shen Te, Brecht goes to extremes here in his depiction of folly, and there should be no suggestion that it does not matter very much after all. Yet the sympathy which Mother Courage does evoke will make its weight felt equally.

For there is a good deal in common in one way or another between this character and Galileo, Puntila, Azdak in *The Caucasian Chalk Circle*, and other of Brecht's outstanding figures. Mother Courage has the shrewdness and wits of Pelagea Vlassova in *The Mother*, though she puts them to a different use. She is adept at turning every situation to her own advantage, conforming with and adapting herself to it in much the same way as Galileo does. She has the vitality of Puntila without his drunkenness or lapses into sobriety, and at the same time she contributes a laconic cynicism of her own, a cunning and ingenuity which are essential for her sheer existence. As a rule she knows exactly how far she can go and how far she can let others go. When the recruiting sergeant threatens to take away her son, she pulls a knife on him, but it is clear that she means the threat as a move in the game, which will not be countered: there is shrewdness in her attitude, not heroism. When the Dutch cook's embrace trickles round into bosom-fondling her rejection of it is determined, but there is a look of wry appraisal in her eye. And do what Brecht might, he could not rewrite the tragic scene, in which she loses her son Swisscheese, in such a way as to destroy all sympathy for her in her grief. Helene Weigel's playing of the part in this scene, consciously styled as it was, would in any case have prevented that. Her dropped jaw, mouth agape with head thrown back and eyes closed, shoulders shrugged and hands lying in the lap,[9] is a purely physical posture that can be adopted without trace of emotion—it is pure "showing," and said to have been copied from a newsreel photograph —but it gripped the mind of the spectator firmly enough for sympathy to be an inevitable outcome.

This is worth noting, since Mother Courage's adaptational successes, so far as they go, are an essential part of the argument of the play, and the sympathy they arouse for her has its part in the total effect. Linking through almost all the scenes, there is in fact a recurrent discussion on the nature of virtue, which her hard-headed opportunism serves to throw into greater prominence. This theme of the virtues is announced from the very beginning, in the opening dialogue between the recruiting officer and his sergeant, and its importance for the whole thus clearly indicated. It is only in war, the soldiers argue —and the irony with which their words are expected to be received quickly becomes apparent—only in war that the virtues flourish. In peace men go to seed; war alone creates order, efficiency, and a sense of responsibility. A little later, Mother Courage herself is heard on the same lines. Bravery and fidelity, strength and ingenuity, she argues, are most needed when things have gone wrong. A bad general needs good troops: "If he was able to make a good plan of campaign, what would he want such brave soldiers for? Ordinary ones would do. Anywhere where there's a lot of virtues, it shows there's something rotten. . . . In a good country there'd be no need of virtues, they could all get half marks for conduct and be cowards for all I care."[10] In fact she warns her children one after another to beware of virtues: Eilif against showing too much bravery, Swisscheese against honesty, Kattrin against love and compassion, and the course of the play demonstrates with increasing intensity how despite her warning each succumbs. Swisscheese is dutifully devoted to his regimental cashbox to the point of suffering torture and death rather than reveal its whereabouts. Eilif is executed for an act of daring which might have earned him a decoration in wartime, but which is thought barbaric in the brief interlude of peace when he happens to commit it. Kattrin dies in a valiant and successful attempt at saving the children of a besieged town from massacre. Thus the sequence of scenes is much less fortuitous than that found in *Puntila*, and a number of them contribute to the argument of the whole. This, indeed, seems to be summed up towards the end in the song of the cook, where the virtues are paraded in verse after verse, and their disastrous consequences shown. The wisdom of Solomon, he sings, ended in the recognition that all was vanity; Caesar's courage was rewarded by the treacherous stab of Brutus; the truthful Socrates was made to drink hemlock, and the charity of St Martin in dividing his cloak merely meant that both he and the beggar froze to death.[11] The cook, it is true, is a rascal who has no business to be decrying qualities he has never tried to show. Yet there is a feeling created by the play of the vanity of all achievement, which makes it very nearly true to say that here, "behind the rational and pragmatic appeal to morality and the argument from morality, lies hidden the cry of all existence: lament at the transitoriness of existence and the futility of human works, good and bad alike."[12] If only that sentence sounded in its context less satisfied, it would hit off Brecht's mood in this play more closely. For there is here, as there is in *The Good Woman*, an emphatic denial that the exercise of virtue is a desirable or an enviable thing.

There is also, however, once again as in *The Good Woman*, a hint of an attitude in which extremes would play no part. To some extent, the play presents the argument that virtues are a product of the warlike lines along which society is run. Where there is competition, there is "war," and in the intervals while new assaults are prepared there is "peace." But the one is intimately bound up with the other. As the army chaplain says, when asked about prospects of peace: "Well, peace! What happens to the hole, when the cheese has been eaten?"[13] Which is a pithier way of putting the Marxist proposition that the oppositions encountered in capitalist society will continue to exist in mutual interpenetration until the qualitative leap has been made into a classless society. There, in a new order, there would be neither peace nor war; since competition would have ceased to exist, the terms would lose meaning, just as we would have no use for terms like "high" and "low" if we had no sense of space. And in the same way the virtues engendered by a competitive world would also cease to exist. "Lucky the man who is free of them," sings the cook. He is thinking perhaps of that millennium in which Brecht continued to believe.

That aspect of the play is underlined when Mother Courage congratulates her daughter on her impediment:

"Be thankful you're dumb, you'll never contradict yourself or want to bite your tongue off because you've told the truth, it's a blessing from God, being dumb is."[14] Yet in the very irony with which she says this—she has only just finished saying, "Love's a power from on high, I'm warning you"—there is a clue to the continuing ambiguity of the work. For while on the one hand virtue is made to look absurd, on the other its value is constantly being reasserted. From an absolute or millennial standpoint, human consistency, truthfulness, fidelity, and the rest are seen as worthless; from a limited standpoint of day-to-day living they are nevertheless presented as high achievements. So it is that in the last scene but one, despite all that has gone before, Kattrin's self-sacrifice on behalf of the besieged city gains added weight. It is introduced by the words included in the prefatory summary projected onto a screen, "The stone begins to speak." She who has lived up till now in an attitude of silent registration of the horrors being perpetrated all round her, emerges from neutrality as Galileo might have emerged from his cunning adaptational opportunism, to set at naught the amorality of a large part of the play. Her protest against the resignation of the peasants, who from cowardice rather than faith can think of no resort but prayer to help the city against attack, acquires the force of a completely natural outburst. The scene has been described as melodramatic.[15] It is certainly one of the two dramatic moments in this otherwise epic play. Yet to be melodramatic it would need to strike a false note, to seem exaggerated in its admiration of heroism, or in some way to inspire a sentimental attitude. It is notoriously difficult to prove a negative—in this case, that there is no such falsity. Yet the thoughtful way in which Kattrin's protest is depicted perhaps indicates sufficiently how little the scene tends in that direction. At first, Kattrin is silent as the Catholic patrol demands to be shown a path through the woods to the city, and even when the peasant's son is blackmailed into acting as a guide she makes no demur. As the father and mother kneel to pray she kneels behind them in unreflecting conformity. It is only when she hears the prayer that the children may be saved that she groans and stands up, as though the direct appeal to her compassion in its tenderest spot suggested a possible action to her. But she acts now in a plain, matter-of-fact spirit, without posturing. Having picked up a drum left by the soldiers and climbed on to the roof of a barn, she takes it so much for granted that the peasants will approve of her conduct that she neglects to draw up the ladder after her until they have almost set foot on it. And in beginning to beat out her alarm to the city she strikes steadily at first, rising to a crescendo only when the returning patrol threatens to shoot her, and her imminent death is certain. The scene, exciting as it is, is not conducted in a spirit of heroics, mock or otherwise. Indeed a mature spirit of just appraisal rules over it even in details. Almost at the last moment, the peasant's son, also returning with the patrol, calls out to Kattrin to go on drumming, and is struck down by a soldier's pike. As the soldier prepares for a second blow the mother casts herself across her son's body: resigned before, she also displays a courage like Kattrin's when her tenderest feelings are aroused. The fairness and restraint of Brecht's presentation do everything possible to avert mere emotionalism.

A similar mood extends into the last scene of all. Mother Courage's body, humped in her ragged padded jacket over the dead Kattrin, must evoke pity. As she marches off again to catch up with a passing regiment, straining in the harness with the wagon behind her, she is bound to arouse admiration for her tenacious perseverance. The lullaby she sings to Kattrin, however, still comforting herself with the illusion that her daughter is alive, is calculated to modify these sentiments, for she sings only of her pleasure that while others suffer her own child is well provided. And her egoism, the source of her tenacity, is stressed again in her last words, "I must get back to business. Take me with you!" The play ends, then, both on this note of tragedy, involving extreme sympathy, and on one of satirical condemnation which excludes any possibility of a sympathy that is merely self-congratulatory or self-pitying. The united elements do indeed provide a drama of a kind never seen before, acknowledging our involvement in human weakness, yet refusing to accept the involvement as final.

To turn from *Mother Courage* to *The Caucasian Chalk Circle*, not written till 1944–5, is to enter a completely different atmosphere, in which, nevertheless, many affinities can still be found. It is as well to say at the outset that the Communistic message which it seems to convey is only loosely connected with the main plot. This is the story of a young Georgian girl, Grusha, who saves the infant child of a tyrannical governor during an insurrection, who brings up the boy until the day when his real mother disputes possession of him before the "good, bad judge" Azdak, and who finally, through the unorthodox wisdom of the judge, is allowed to retain the child because she alone has shown a true motherly nature. It scarcely follows from this that (as the epilogue suggests) the Soviet authorities are entitled to deprive industrious dairy-farming peasants of their land in order to hand it over to others who will make use of it for viniculture. And the prologue, in which this contemporary problem is outlined (the play itself being performed as a means of persuading the reluctant dairy-farmers to yield), is remarkable for the prim diction of the Soviet officials, the conventional picture it gives of shrewd, but good-hearted peasants, and the "socialist realism" of its style and presentation.

All this is in contrast to the non-naturalistic, many-sided, lyrical, humorous, Rabelaisian, socially conscious elements of the "play within the play." The girl Grusha is not in the least conventionally drawn, though she too is shrewd and good-hearted. We do not sit back in uncomfortable or smug contentment telling ourselves that this is what sturdy peasants are really like, as we are invited to do in the prologue. She shows considerable courage in crossing a rickety bridge over a mountain chasm while being pursued by insurrectionist soldiers; she combines this with artfulness, a ready wit, blunt honesty, stubborn insistence, and an unshakable moral probity. When she is married for convenience sake to a dying man who will be at least a nominal father for the child she has saved, and when the man, a skrimshanker, rises from his "deathbed" on hearing that the war is over, she continues to pay him a wifely respect, shows no resentment or self-pity. When, later, her lover Simon to whom she is betrothed returns from the war, she allows him to suspect her of infidelity rather than betray the child to its enemies. Courage, perseverance, motherliness, dutifulness, self-sacrifice she shows time and again. Yet because of her equanimity and lack of self-regard, these qualities have no false ring. And this is due also in part to the deliberately non-naturalistic language she speaks. Brecht makes no attempt to reproduce peasant speech faithfully: Grusha's is sprinkled with proverbs and dialect forms, but it also includes direct translations of English idiom; when she sings a lullaby to the child it is at once a song that vividly recalls ancient German folk-art and at the same time has a modern ring. Subtly and continuously through the language Brecht persuades us not quite to believe in Grusha, to accept her as a creation of art, and to look beyond her to a reality which in part we re-create ourselves. The formality of his presentation reaches its climax in the scene, concluding the first part of Grusha's adventures, where Simon returns and speaks with her across a river that separates them. The lovers address each other at first in an exchange of proverbs which is both humorous and characteristic of their peasant origins. It is also, however, quite impersonal, a drawing on common tradition, and it is only by reflexion that the deep personal relationship between them is felt. In the climactic moment of the scene, in fact, neither speaks, and it is left to the narrator to reveal what each "thought, but did not say." Thus they confront each other in formal attitudes which are never realistically portrayed but are at the same time deeply moving, and it is by a similar estrangement that Brecht succeeds in making the outstanding human qualities of Grusha credible and acceptable.

The scenes of Grusha's escape, adventures, marriage, and rejection by Simon, forming about half the play, make a loosely-strung narrative in the fashion of "epic" theatre. While there is a certain thread connecting them, however—they do not stand "each for themselves," as Brecht suggested earlier that "epic" scenes should do[16]—the interest is sustained not so much by the thin plot as by the detailed interactions of the characters[17] and by the beauty of the portrayal. Since *Baal*, Brecht had scarcely made any use in his plays of the natural scene. In *The Caucasian Chalk Circle*, as in *Puntila* and *The Good Woman* and in his later poetry, the world of nature returns. The scene by the river itself, indicated on the stage merely by two ground-rows of reeds, evokes by its bareness, coupled with the lyrical song of the narrator preceding it, an awareness of loveliness. The icicles above Grusha's hut, as she waits in isolation for the winter to pass, become moving tokens of spring as they melt, and the musical notes of a xylophone offstage, recording the falling drops of water, add excitement by their rising intensity. There is time for contemplation and for exhilaration in these austerely presented moments; the spectator is not whirled along as he was by the action of earlier plays, and not encouraged to indulge in ecstatic Nature-worship, but rather to recognise with pleasure the delight that is to be had from Nature, off the stage. There is both detachment and attachment.

The settings also, in this part of the play, evoke an astringent delight. The descending white back-cloth has already been mentioned. There is also the scene of Grusha's wedding, contrived to give a Breughelesque harmony of brown, oatmeal, sepia, has an occasional splash of red: peasant colours in a peasant setting, crowded, earthy, vulgarly frank, but shaped into a frame of unity that is comic, sympathetic, and has a lop-sided symmetry of its own. There is the strange effect of the empty stage after the insurrection has passed by, with the voice of the narrator emerging from one side to comment on the silence and thereby, oddly enough, to intensify it. Meanwhile, from time to time, the prose speech breaks into verse such as that in which Grusha affirms her love at Simon's first departure:

> Simon Chachava, I will wait for you.
> Go in good heart to the battle, soldier,
> The bloody battle, the bitter battle
> From which not all come back:
> When you come back, I will be there.
> I will wait for you under the green elm
> I will wait for you under the bare elm
> I will wait till the last man comes back
> And longer.
> When you come back from the battle
> No boots will stand by the door
> The pillow by mine will be empty
> And my mouth unkissed.
> When you come back, when you come back
> You can say it is all as it was.[18]

It comes as a shock to go on from this moving language and these scenes to the following series which forgets Grusha entirely in order to introduce the story of the judge Azdak. From Azdak's first speech, the spectator is hit by a forceful language which English can barely reproduce: "Schnaub nicht, du bist kein Gaul. Und es hilft dir nicht bei der Polizei, wenn du läufst, wie ein Rotz im April. Steh, sag ich. . . . Setz dich nieder und futtre, da ist ein Stück Käse. Lang nichts gefressen? Warum bist du gerannt, du Arschloch?"[19] The crudity of this, the rough vigour, the cynicism and humour and the underlying sympathy introduce the character of Azdak himself, which stands in strange contrast to Grusha's. Azdak is a thief, a time-server, a coward, who by a lucky accident is raised during the insurrection to a position of authority. As a judge he is corrupt, licentious, contemptuous of law and order, a lickspittle. His life is spent, unlike Grusha's, not in rebellious opposition to society's moral standards, but in careful adaptation to them, going along with the tide, and keeping an eye on the main chance. But such an account does less than justice to this unpredictable rogue. In the first scene, finding that the poor man he thought he was sheltering is in fact the Grand Duke, fleeing from the insurrection, he still does not hand him over to the police, although whether from sheer contempt for the police, as he says, or contempt for the Duke, or from an inscrutable sympathy such as Ernst Busch implies when he plays him, is never clear. Promptly, he rushes into town to denounce himself, believing that the soldiery will welcome the news of his treachery—some strange conscientiousness is at work in him. Yet on discovering them to be indifferent to the rights and wrongs of the insurrection, he willingly allows them to clothe him in judicial robes, and goes off on his rampaging procession through the countryside, delivering sentences that completely reverse accepted standards of justice. He accepts bribes, but (though he keeps the money) only as an indication of the wealth of the litigants, which stands in his eyes in inverse proportion to their rights. He makes an award in favour of a poor woman who has been helped by a bandit, on the grounds that only a miracle could explain how a leg of pork came to fly through a poor woman's window: those who accuse the bandit of stealing the pork and throwing it through the window are condemned for godlessness and disbelief in miracles. When a buxom young woman accuses a farmhand of rape, he considers her luxurious gait and the shape of her buttocks and finds her guilty of assault and battery with a dangerous weapon, after which he goes off with her to "examine the scene of the crime." And when order is re-established he falls over himself with dutiful promises that Grusha, whom he has not yet met, shall be beheaded as soon as she is found.

Azdak is a standing affront, and at the same time a standing reminder of the questionable values on which society is based. He has one principle, that the rights of the poor are disregarded and that this situation must be reversed. Apart from that, he proceeds *ad hoc*. If a buxom girl is likely to commit rape he offers her the opportunity. On the other hand, if he foresees danger in maintaining his one principle, he gives way immediately: "I'm not doing any one the favour of showing human greatness." Yet all this is not mere self-gratification or concern for his own skin. There is nothing that can properly be called a self in Azdak, nothing consistent or foreseeable in his actions: he acts on impulse. He sets no store by his actions, any more than Grusha does by hers, and it is this that helps to make him the most fascinating character in the play, insulting and generous, preposterous and humble, ignorant and wise, blasphemous and pious. In his Villonesque song to the poor woman he addresses her as though she were the Virgin Mary and begs mercy for such damned creatures as himself—a strange translation from religious into human terms which still has an atmosphere of genuine devoutness. In the scene where he is buffeted in his false robes by the soldiery, the production of the Berliner Ensemble is deliberately styled to recall another buffeting. And in the comment of the narrator there is a further suggestion of a wider scope: "And so he broke the laws, as he broke bread, that it might feed them."[20] The suggestion need not be taken too far. Yet there is in Azdak, the scandal, the gnome, the cynical good-liver, something immensely disturbing and provocative as well as attractive. He denies all the virtues, mocks at repentance and charity, ridicules courage, and, strangely enough, he gets our sympathy in the process. For he is plainly being himself to the top of his bent, lusting and helping the poor, crawling in abject fear and at the same time inviting the soldiers to recognise their own doglike obedience, answering every prompting with instinctive recklessness. If we give him our sympathy, as we cannot help doing, in a way, so long as he dominates the stage, he sets all Grusha's virtuousness at naught. This is Baal, returned to the scene in a new guise, and all Baal's fascination pours out from him.

In the final scene of all, the two sides are confronted with one another, the disruptive, ambiguous underminer and the calm, shrewd, motherly girl who would rather die than forego her humanity. Azdak is called to try the case in which the real mother of Grusha's "child," the wife of the former governor of the province, claims possession of her son. By a fortunate turn of events, the same Grand Duke whose life Azdak saved earlier on has now returned to power, and thus Azdak's servile promise to the governor's wife no longer has any hold over him, if indeed he ever meant to keep it. Azdak proceeds, however, as usual, accepting bribes from the wealthier party, while abusing Simon and Grusha who have nothing to offer him, and it is this which brings on the first serious opposition he has had to encounter. Grusha declares that she has no respect for a judge such as he is, "no more than I have for a thief and a murderer that does what he likes."[21] Her moral protest is a straightforward indictment of his libertinism (which is no mere show), and none the worse for that; in fact she has all, or nearly all, our sympathy. Yet the end will have already been guessed. After the "trial of the chalk circle" in which each woman is to pull at the child from different sides, and Grusha fails to pull for fear of hurting the boy, Azdak ceremonially declares that Grusha is the true mother since she alone has shown true motherly feelings. This is not, however, a sentimental ending awarding victory to justice against the run of the odds. Rather, it is the fusion of two conceptions of justice. Azdak's instinctive prompting on this occasion (he is, after all, in safety now, with the governor's wife in political disgrace) is to award Grusha the custody of the child. But this instinctive prompting is a part of his elemental originality, his closeness to the roots of his nature, and his complete detachment from them. His decision has gathered the weight and incontrovertibility of a natural phenomenon, and despite his mockery of the virtues here is one virtue in Grusha that he respects without thought of argument.

Thus the two sides come together. Like Nietzsche, Azdak demands opposition such as he gets from Grusha, and thrives on it. Like Nature itself, he is ambiguous and amoral and requires the rebelliousness of humanity to bring out his qualities to the full. Then, however, when he meets with opposition, he reveals an unexpected generosity (as Nietzsche never did). He is like Baal, it is true. But Baal was never opposed, lived his life in pure self-fulfilment, and died only to the tune of contempt from others. Azdak is Baal, and all that lies behind Baal, brought into relationship with human beings, and this relationship and conflict serve to make *The Caucasian Chalk Circle* far greater in scope than its predecessor. The virtue of Grusha is both convincingly stated and brought into question, the amoralism of Azdak is made to look both repugnant and curiously attractive, and yet in the final moments a fusion of Grusha's human demands and Azdak's inhuman unpredictability brings about a sense of at least temporary fulfilment. As the narrator has it, the period of Azdak's life as a judge could be looked back upon as "a brief Golden Age almost of justice." It was not *the* Golden Age, and it was not a time of complete justice. Both Azdak and Grusha have been too "estranged" for us to be able to accept them as models or heroes. But while steering clear of absolutes Brecht creates here an ending which is satisfying on a purely human plane. Despite the riotous exaggeration of a great part of the play, from which he never recants for an instant, the conclusion is moderately and accurately stated.

These five later plays show Brecht at his best. He was able in them to give full vent to that tendency in him to take every situation to its extreme—the tendency that caused him to paint the soldiers' faces in *Edward II* chalk-white, and to expect acquiescence in the outrageous conclusions of *The Measures Taken*—but the extremes are balanced now one against the other. The weaknesses in his plays continue to arise when he becomes, as he himself would have put it, "undialectical"—in other words, when he allows scope only to one aspect of the dialectical opposites inherent in human nature. On his return to Eastern Germany, such weaknesses increased, as his version of *Antigone* and the adaptation from George Farquhar clearly show. Within that atmosphere, he found increasing encouragement to become fixed in his political views, and on the whole his plays suffered accordingly. But while he was able, for a time, to live himself out to the full in his plays, his work gained an immediacy of impact which communicates itself regardless of nation and class. He is best remembered for the intensity of his probing into moral and social problems, the wisdom which shows itself in his willingness to utilise every condition and limitation of the theatre in such a way as to reflect immediately on the conditions and limitations of living, the purification of his compassion from self-flattering benevolence to matter-of-fact cognisance of human needs, and the abundant vitality of many of his central characters. To the end, this vitality tended to be restricted to a small number of his creations: only in *The Caucasian Chalk Circle*, and particularly in *Mother Courage*, does it spill over into a wide range of personalities. But in these two, especially in the full life given to them by Brecht's own productions, the many facets of his work, realised from time to time in the earlier as in the latest plays, are concentrated in dramatic unities that come very close to expressing the whole man.

REFERENCES

1. *S.*, xi, pp. 388–9.
2. Esslin, p. 264.
3. *S.*, vii, p. 154.
4. *S.*, vii, p. 90.
5. Mennemeier, p. 400.
6. *Ibid.*
7. Quoted in Esslin, p. 204.
8. Esslin, p. 205.
9. Photographs in *T.*, p. 265.
10. *S.*, vii, pp. 89–90.
11. *S.*, vii, pp. 185–8.
12. Mennemeier, p. 392.
13. *S.*, vii, p. 147.
14. *S.*, vii, p. 98.
15. See p. 28 above.
16. See p. 63 above.
17. See p. 30 above.
18. *S.*, x, p. 164.
19. *S.*, x, p. 237.
20. *S.*, x, p. 271.
21. *S.*, x, p. 293.

BIBLIOGRAPHY

I. BRECHT'S WORKS

The most extensive and reliable bibliography of Brecht is that by Walter Nubel in *Sinn und Form*, Zweites Sonderheft Bertolt Brecht, Berlin, 1957. Other bibliographical data are given in the first "Sonderheft" of the same periodical, and in the works by J. Willett, M. Esslin and M. Kesting, details of which appear below. The author is indebted to all these in his compilation of the following lists.

There are three collected editions of Brecht's works, none of them complete. The earliest, the *Versuche* (here cited as *V.*), began in 1930 and now runs to 15 vols., in addition to a special unnumbered "Sonderheft." Published by Suhrkamp, Berlin, it contains 21 plays, some poems, and various prose writings. The second collection was the *Gesammelte Werke*, published by Malik Verlag, London, in 1938. This ceased after two volumes had appeared, and contains twelve plays. The third collection was the *Stücke* (here cited as *S.*), begun in 1955 by Suhrkamp, Berlin, which in 1960 has 12 vols. containing 34 plays and some dramatic theory and comment. (A slightly different edition with the same title is published by Aufbauverlag, Berlin.) For the present study, the text of the plays given in *S.* has been taken as standard, and for the theoretical writings, that given in *V.*

The first volume of a collection of plays by Brecht in translation (here cited as *P.*) has now been published by Messrs Methuen. *Seven Plays by Bertolt Brecht*, tr. E. Bentley *et al.* (Grove Press 1961; here cited as *S.P.*) contains a long introduction by E. Bentley.

1. Plays

All plays are to be found in *S.*, unless otherwise stated. They are arranged here in chronological order of writing. The first date after the title, in brackets, is that of the first performance in German, the second is that of the first German edition.

Baal (=*Baal*), (Leipzig 1923) Potsdam 1922.

Drums in the Night (=*Trommeln in der Nacht*), (Munich 1922) Munich 1923.

In the Cities' Jungle (=*Im Dickicht der Städte*), (Munich 1923) Berlin 1927. As *In the Swamp*, tr. E. Bentley, in *S.P.*

Edward II (=*Leben Eduards II von England*; after Marlowe), (Munich 1924) Potsdam 1924.

A Man's a Man (=*Mann ist Mann*), (Darmstadt 1926) Berlin 1927. Tr. E. Bentley, in *S.P.*

The Baby Elephant (=*Das Elefantenkalb*), (Darmstadt 1926?) Berlin 1927. Tr. G. Nellhaus in *Wake*, No. 8, Aut. 1949.

The Threepenny Opera (=*Die Dreigroschenoper*; after Gay), (Berlin 1928) Vienna 1929. Tr. E. Bentley and D. Vesey in *The Modern Theatre*, I, Doubleday Anchor Books, 1955, and in *P.*, I.

Rise and Fall of the Town of Mahagonny (=*Aufstieg und Fall der Stadt Mahagonny*), (Leipzig 1930) Vienna 1929.

The Flight over the Ocean (=*Der Ozeanflug*, originally *Der Flug der Lindberghs*). Not in *S.* (Baden-Baden 1929) Berlin 1930 in *V.*, I. Tr. G. Antheil, Universal-Edition, Vienna 1930.

Baden-Baden Cantata of Acquiescence (=*Das Badener Lehrstück vom Einverständnis*), (Baden-Baden 1929) Berlin 1930 in *V.*, II. Tr. G. Nellhaus in *Harvard Advocate*, CXXXIV. 4 (Feb. 1951).

St. Joan of the Stockyards (=*Die heilige Johanna der Schlachthöfe*), (Hamburg 1959) Berlin 1932 in *V.*, V. Tr. F. Jones in *From the Modern Repertoire*, ed. E. Bentley, Indiana University Press 1956, and in *S.P.*

He who said Yes/He who said No (=*Der Jasager/Der Neinsager*) (*Der Jasager* only, Berlin 1930) Berlin 1930. Tr. G. Nellhaus in *Accent* (Urbana) VII, 2 (Aut. 1946).

The Measures Taken (=*Die Massnahme*), (Berlin 1930) Berlin 1931 in *V.*, IV. Tr. E. Bentley in *The Colorado Review*, I, 1, Wint. 1956–7.

The Exception and the Rule (=*Die Ausnahme und die Regel*), (Paris 1947) Moscow 1937. Tr. E. Bentley in *Chrysalis* (Boston), Dec. 1954, and in *New Directions* (New York), XV (1955).

The Mother (=*Die Mutter*; after Gorki's novel), (Berlin 1932) Berlin 1933 in *V.*, VII.

The Horatii and the Curiatii (=*Die Horatier und die Kuriatier*). (Halle/Wittenberg 1958). London 1938 in Malik edn. of *Werke*. Tr. H. R. Hays in *Accent* (Urbana), VIII, 1 (Aut. 1947).

Round Heads and Pointed Heads (=*Die Rundköpfe und die Spitzköpfe*), (Copenhagen 1936) London 1938 in Malik edn. of *Werke*. Tr. N. G. Verschoyle in *International Literature* (Moscow), May 1937.

The Seven Deadly Sins (=*Die Sieben Todsünden*, also called *Anna-Anna*). (Paris 1933). German text and tr. on the sleeve of American recording, Columbia KL 5175, also on Phillips recording B 07186 L. Not in *S.*

The Private Life of the Master Race (=*Furcht und Elend des dritten Reiches*), (Paris 1938) Moscow 1941. Tr. E. Bentley, New York 1944, and London 1948. Also tr. as *Fear and Misery in the Third Reich*, publ. Mezhdunarodnaya Kniga, Moscow 1942.

Señora Carrar's Rifles (=*Die Gewehre der Frau Carrar*; after Synge), (Paris 1937) London 1937. Tr. K. Wallis in *Theatre Workshop* (New York), II (1938).

Mother Courage and her Children (=*Mutter Courage und ihre Kinder*),

(Zürich 1941) Frankfurt 1949 in *V.*, IX. Tr. H. R. Hays in *New Directions* (Norfolk) 1941; and E. Bentley in *The Modern Theatre*, II, New York 1955, and in *S.P.*

The Life of Galileo (=*Leben des Galilei*), (Zürich 1943) Berlin 1955 in *V.*, XIV. Tr. Brecht and C. Laughton in *From the Modern Repertoire*, II, ed. E. Bentley, Denver U.P. 1952, and in *S.P.*; and D. I. Vesey in *P.*, I.

The Trial of Lucullus (=*Das Verhör des Lukullus*), (Berne radio 1940) Moscow 1940. Tr. H. R. Hays, New York 1943, and in *P.*, I.

The Condemnation of Lucullus (=*Die Verurteilung des Lukullus*), (Berlin 1951) Berlin and Zürich 1951.

The Good Woman of Setzuan (=*Der gute Mensch von Sezuan*), (Zürich 1943) Berlin 1953 in *V.*, XII. Tr. E. and M. Bentley in *Parables for the Theatre*, Minnesota 1948 and Oxford 1948, also in Evergreen Books, Grove Press, New York, and in *S.P.*

Herr Puntila and his Man Matti (=*Herr Puntila und sein Knecht Matti*; after stories by Wuolijoki). (Zürich 1948) Munich 1948. Scenes 9 and 11 tr. R. Grenier and G. Nellhaus in *Accent* (Urbana), XIV, 2 (Spr. 1954).

The Resistible Ascent of Arturo Ui (=*Der aufhaltsame Aufstieg des Arturo Ui*). (Stuttgart 1958) in *SF.* 2.

The Visions of Simone Machard (=*Die Gesichte der Simone Machard*). (Frankfurt 1957) in *Sinn und Form*, nos. 5–6, Potsdam 1956.

Schweik in the Second World War (=*Schweyk im zweiten Weltkrieg*). (Erfurt 1958) Frankfurt 1957 in *S.*, X.

The Caucasian Chalk Circle (=*Der Kaukasische Kreidekreis*). (Berlin 1954) Potsdam 1949 in *SF.* I. Tr. E. and M. Bentley in *Parables for the Theatre*, Minnesota 1948 and Oxford 1948; also in Evergreen Books, Grove Press, New York, and in *S.P.* Also tr. J. and T. Stern with W. H. Auden in *P.*, I.

Antigone (=*Die Antigone des Sophokles*). (Chur 1948) in *Antigonemodell 1948*, Berlin 1949.

The Days of the Commune (=*Die Tage der Commune*). (Karl Marx-Stadt 1956) Berlin 1957 in *V.*, XV.

The Tutor (=*Der Hofmeister*; after Lenz). (Berlin 1950) Berlin 1951 in *V.*, XI.

Report from Herrnburg (=*Herrnburger Bericht*). (Berlin 1951) in *Neues Deutschland*, Berlin, 22 Jul. 1951; not in *S.*

Coriolanus (=*Coriolan*; after Shakespeare). (not yet performed in 1960) Frankfurt 1959 in *S.*, XI.

The Trial of Joan of Arc (=*Der Prozess der Jeanne d'Arc zu Rouen 1431*; after Seghers). (Berlin 1952) Frankfurt 1959 in *S.*, XII.

Don Juan (=*Don Juan*; after Molière, in collaboration with B. Besson and E. Hauptmann). (Rostock 1952) Frankfurt 1959 in *S.*, XII.

Drums and Trumpets (=*Pauken und Trompeten*; after Farquhar, in collaboration with B. Besson and E. Hauptmann). (Berlin 1955) Frankfurt 1959 in *S.*, XII.

Further unpublished or unfinished plays are listed in Willett, pp. 26, 30, 33, 58–61.

2. *Poetry*

Bertolt Brecht, Selected Poems. Tr. H. R. Hays, Evergreen Books, Grove Press, New York, and John Calder, London, 1959 (originally New York, 1947).

Brecht's poems are scattered in many places, a large number of them in *V.* and *S.F.* Outside these collections, the principal vols. are:

Bertolt Brechts Taschenpostille. Privately printed 1926; new edition, Berlin 1958.

Bertolt Brechts Hauspostille. Berlin 1927; new edition Frankfurt 1951.

Gedichte, Lieder, Chöre. Paris 1934.

Svendborger Gedichte. London 1939.

Die Erziehung der Hirse. Berlin 1951.

Recent anthologies include the following:

Bertolt Brechts Gedichte und Lieder. Selected by Peter Suhrkamp. Berlin and Frankfurt 1956. Recommended.

Bertolt Brecht. Gedichte. Selected by Siegfried Streller, Leipzig 1955 (=Reclams Universal-Bibliothek no. 7996/97).

3. *Prose-Fiction*

A Penny for the Poor (=*Der Dreigroschenroman*). Tr. D. I. Vesey and C. Isherwood, London 1937. Reprinted as *Threepenny Novel*, Evergreen Books, Grove Press, New York 1956, and Bernard Hanison, London 1958.

The Business Deals of Mr Julius Caesar (=*Die Geschäfte des Herrn Julius Cäsar*). Extract tr. by D. Alexander in *Nimbus New English Review* (London) IV, 2 (1958).

Meditations of Herr Keuner (=selection from *Geschichten vom Herrn Keuner*), tr. H. Fraenkel in *The New Statesman*, London, 3 Nov. 1956.

Calendar Tales (=*Kalendergeschichten*), Berlin 1948.

For further details, see Esslin, pp. 275–9.

4. *Films*

For details of Brecht's share in films, see Willett, p. 262.

5. *Dramatic Theory*

"A Little Organum for the Theatre" (="Kleines Organon für das Theater"), tr. B. Gottlieb in *Accent* (Urbana) XI, I (Wint. 1951).

"A Model for Epic Acting" (="Die Strassenszene"), tr. E. Bentley in *The Sewanee Review*, Jul.–Sep. 1959.

"A New Technique of Acting" (="Neue Technik der Schauspielkunst"), tr. E. Bentley in *Theatre Arts* (New York), Jan. 1949 and in *New Theatre* (London), Mar. 1949.

"Notes to the Threepenny Opera" (also Brecht's notes on *Galileo* and *Lucullus*) in *P.* I.

A large number of Brecht's theoretical writings will be found in his *Schriften zum Theater*, Berlin and Frankfurt 1957. See also the "modelbooks," with numerous pictures of Brecht's productions, e.g. *Antigonemodell 1948*, *Couragemodell 1949*, and especially *Theaterarbeit, Sechs Aufführungen des Berliner Ensembles*, Dresden 1952.

II. STUDIES

1. *In English*

ADLER, HENRY: "Bert Brecht's Theatre," in *The Twentieth Century*, 160 (1956), pp. 114–23.

BENTLEY, ERIC R.: *The Playwright as Thinker*, New York 1946 (= *The Modern Theatre*, London 1948).

——: *In Search of Theater*, New York 1953 and London 1954, pp. 141–60, 390–3.

ESSLIN, MARTIN: *Brecht, a Choice of Evils*, London 1959.

——: "Bertolt Brecht—'A Choice of Evils'," in *The Manchester Guardian*, 26 Nov. 1959 (a reply to John Willett).

GRAY, RONALD: "Mother Courage" in *Cambridge Review*, 20 Oct. 1956.

GREENBERG, CLEMENT: "Bertolt Brecht's Poetry," in *Partisan Review*, VIII (Mar.–Apr. 1941), pp. 114–27.

HAYS, H. R.: "The Poetry of Bertolt Brecht," in *Poetry*, LXVII. (Dec. 1945), pp. 148–55.

LUETHY, HERBERT: "Of Poor Bert Brecht," in *Encounter* 34 (Jul. 1956), pp. 33–53.

TRETYAKOV, SERGEI: "Bert Brecht," in *International Literature*, No. 5, May 1937, pp. 60–70.

TYNAN, KENNETH: "Brecht and the German Theatre," in *The New Yorker*, 12 Sep. 1959.

VIERTEL, BERTHOLD: "Bertolt Brecht, dramatist," in *The Kenyon Review*, VII (1945), pp. 467–75.

WILLETT, JOHN: *The Theatre of Bertolt Brecht*, London 1959.

——: "Thoughts on Brechtian Theatre," in *Adam and Encore*, Brecht number, 1956.

——: "The Complexity of Bertolt Brecht," in *The Manchester Guardian*, 12 Nov. 1959 (a criticism of Martin Esslin's book).

2. *In German and French*

BENJAMIN, WALTER: "Was ist episches Theater?" in *Akzente* (Munich), Apr. 1954, pp. 163–70.

BUNGE, HANS JOACHIM: "Brecht probiert," in *S.F.* 2 (details below).

FASSMANN, KURT: *Bert Brecht, eine Bildbiographie*, Munich 1958.

GRIMM, REINHOLD: *Bertolt Brecht. Die Struktur seines Werkes*, Nuremberg 1957.

HINCK, WALTER: *Die Dramaturgie des späten Brecht* (*Palaestra*, No. 229), Göttingen 1959.

IHERING, HERBERT: *Berliner Dramaturgie*, Berlin 1947.

JUSOWSKI, JOSEF: "Bertolt Brecht und sein 'Guter Mensch'," in *S.F.* 2 (details below).

KESTING, MARIANNE: *Bertolt Brecht, dargestellt in Selbstzeugnissen und Bilddokumenten*, Hamburg 1959.

KLOTZ, VOLKER: *Bertolt Brecht. Versuch über das Werk*, Darmstadt 1957.

LUKACS, GEORG: *Skizze einer Geschichte der neueren deutschen Literatur*, Berlin 1955, pp. 141–2.

MANN, OTTO: *B.B.—Mass oder Mythos? Ein kritischer Beitrag über die Schaustücke Bertolt Brechts*, Heidelberg 1958.

MENNEMEIER, FRANZ N.: "Brecht: *Mutter Courage und ihre Kinder*," in *Das Deutsche Drama*, ed. B. von Wiese, Düsseldorf 1958, II. 383–400.

ROHRMOSER, GÜNTER: "Brecht: *Das Leben des Galilei*," in *Das Deutsche Drama*, ed. B. von Wiese, Düsseldorf 1958, II. 401–14.

SARTRE, JEAN-PAUL: "Brecht et les classiques," in *World Theatre* (Paris), VII, 1 (Spr. 1958).

SCHÖNE, ALBRECHT: "Brecht: 'Erinnerung an die Marie A.' " in *Die Deutsche Lyrik*, ed. B. von Wiese, Düsseldorf 1956, II. 485–94.

——: "Bertolt Brecht. Theatertheorie und dramatische Dichtung," in *Euphorion*, LII (1958), pp. 272 ff.

SCHUMACHER, ERNST: *Die dramatischen Versuche Bertolt Brechts 1918–1933*, Berlin 1955.

SERREAU, GENEVIÈVE: *Bertolt Brecht*, Paris 1954.

SZONDI, PETER: *Theorie des modernen Dramas*, Frankfurt 1956.

WINTZEN, RENÉ: *Bertolt Brecht*, Paris 1954.

WIRTH, ANDRZEJ: "Über die stereometrische Struktur der Brechtschen Stücke," in *S.F.* 2 (details below).

ZWERENZ, GERHARD: *Aristotelische und Brechtsche Dramatik*, Rudolstadt 1956.

See also:

Sinn und Form, Sonderheft Bertolt Brecht, ed. J. R. Becher and P. Wiegler, Berlin, n.d. (=*S.F.* 1).

Sinn und Form, Zweites Sonderheft Bertolt Brecht, ed. Die deutsche Akademie der Künste, Berlin, 1957 (=*S.F.* 2).